ARTISANAL SMALL-BATCH

Brewing

ARTISANAL SMALL-BATCH

># Brewing

EASY HOMEMADE WINES, BEERS, MEADS AND CIDERS

Amber Shehan, FOUNDER OF PIXIE'S POCKET

PAGE STREET
PUBLISHING CO.

PAGE STREET
PUBLISHING CO.

First published in 2019 by

Page Street Publishing Co.

27 Congress Street, Suite 105

Salem, MA 01970

www.pagestreetpublishing.com

Distributed by Macmillan, sales in Canada by The Canadian Manda Group.

22   21   20   19   18   1   2   3   4   5

ISBN-13: 978-1-62414-781-4

ISBN-10: 1-62414-781-X

Library of Congress Control Number: 2018968070

Cover and book design by Laura Gallant for Page Street Publishing Co.

Photography by Jen CK Jacobs

Printed and bound in the United States

For Eric and Alia,
my dearest loves

Contents

INTRODUCTION — 9
BREWING BASICS — 11
    WHY ONE-GALLON BATCHES? — 12
    SUGGESTED EQUIPMENT FOR BEGINNERS — 12
    YEAST AND OTHER INGREDIENTS — 16
    THE BASIC BREWING PROCESS — 18

The Gift of the Bees — 20
HEAVENLY HONEY MEAD

IT'S ALL ABOUT THE HONEY — 21
MASTER RECIPE: BASIC MEAD — 23
    LOVELY LEMON BALM MEAD — 27
    WILDFLOWER MEAD — 28
    BLUEBERRY MUFFIN MEAD — 31
    ROSEMARY AND CLEMENTINE MEAD — 32
    GOLDEN MEAD — 35
    ROSE PETAL AND HIBISCUS MEAD — 36
    VANILLA BEAN AND CHAMOMILE MEAD — 39
    LEMON AND GINGER MEAD — 40
    BLACK CHERRY MEAD — 43
    HONEYMOON MEAD — 44
    CYSER (APPLE MEAD) — 47
    PYMENT (GRAPE MEAD) — 48

Vintage Varietals — 50
FRUIT AND COUNTRY WINES

LET'S DEFINE "WINE" — 51
MASTER RECIPE: FRUIT WINE — 53
    SPICED POMEGRANATE WINE — 57
    PINEAPPLE WINE — 58
    HONEYSUCKLE WINE — 61
    PEPPERMINT WINE — 62
    ELDERBERRY AND ROSE HIP WINE — 65
    STRAWBERRY AND LINDEN FLOWER WINE — 66
    GRAPEFRUIT WINE — 69
    SCARBOROUGH FAIR WINE — 70
    EARL GREY TEA WINE — 73
    FRUITCAKE WINE — 74
    RASPBERRY-PEAR WINE — 77
    CHOCOLATE-CHERRY WINE — 78

Johnny-Jump-Up 80

CIDERS SWEET AND DRY

AN APPLE A DAY . . .   81
MASTER RECIPE: BASIC CIDER   83
   PERRY (PEAR CIDER)   87
   ORANGE-HIBISCUS CIDER   88
   DARK GINGER CIDER   91
   MAPLE SYRUP CIDER   92
   CHAI-SPICED CIDER   95
   SUMMER BERRY CIDER   96
   DRY-HOPPED CIDER   99
   FLOWER GARDEN CIDER   100
   ROSE CIDER   103
   MALTED CIDER   104

Grains and Gruits and Hops, Oh My! 106

TO HOP, OR NOT TO HOP?   107
MASTER RECIPE: AMERICAN PILSNER   109
   GRUIT ALE   113
   CHERRY RED ALE   114
   THYME AND HONEY SAISON   117
   ROOT BEER BROWN ALE   118
   LEMON-PEPPER IPA   121
   BASIL TRIPEL   122
   APRICOT AMERICAN WHEAT BEER   125
   BLUEBERRY PORTER   126
   ELDERFLOWER PALE ALE   129
   DEEP ROOTS CHOCOLATE STOUT   130
   MUGWORT BEER   133
   BRAGGOT   134

Beyond the Brews 137

COCKTAILS   139
   MEAD SPRITZER   139
   MULLED MEAD, WINE AND CIDER   140
   MULLED RED WINE OR CIDER   140
   MULLED MEAD OR WHITE WINE   140
SIMPLE SYRUPS   143
   BASIC SIMPLE SYRUP   143
   GINGER-HONEY SYRUP   144
   CINNAMON-BROWN SUGAR SYRUP   147
COOKING WITH HOMEBREWS   148
   SPENT-GRAIN FLOUR   148
   HERBED SPENT-GRAIN CRACKERS   151
   SPENT-GRAIN GRANOLA   152
   SPENT-GRAIN BEER BREAD   155
   MARINADES AND SAUCES   156
   VINAIGRETTES   159
   BOOZY JELLIES   160
   CIDER-POACHED PEARS   163
   FRUIT-SCRAP VINEGAR   164

ACKNOWLEDGMENTS   167
ABOUT THE AUTHOR   169
INDEX   170

INTRODUCTION

I recall my first taste of mead as if it were yesterday. The homebrewed honey wine was delightfully sweet and the rich complexity of flavors rolling over my tongue left me dazed! Soon after that, I tasted my first homebrewed Concord grape wine, a sharp and sweet brew that could easily give you the worst hangover in the world if you dared to overindulge. Next came a strawberry wine so thick and rich that it felt like you were drinking a smoothie. Bit by bit, I fell in love.

These hand-crafted brews were so much more alive, nuanced and unique than the mass-produced wines and beers that I was familiar with, and I knew at a taste that I must learn how to wield the magic of creating such exciting concoctions!

I began my path as an herbalist around the same time as I experienced those first tastes of homebrewed beverages. The two worlds intertwined beautifully, and I've never looked back! My knowledge of herbs and their properties has helped to inspire some of my best brews.

Herbs have been included in brewing for centuries: from Babylonian beer recipes chanted by priestesses in honor of Ninkasi, the Sumerian goddess of beer, to the traditional gruit ales made before hops were so commonplace. Even today, many breweries in the modern craft beer scene incorporate exotic herbs and revive ancient recipes in an exploration of flavor and techniques.

These days, my garden, hedgerow, local brew shop and farmers' markets supply me with everything I need to pursue the craft of brewing. A bounty of culinary and medicinal herbs can be used to make brews both intoxicating and tonic. The excess fruits of the harvest can be preserved for out-of-season enjoyment—just imagine the delight of opening a bottle of blueberry mead on an icy winter's day!

I truly hope that this book helps inspire you to learn to brew up your own bounties. It is a joy and a delight to crack open a bottle of something special that you created and share it with friends and family. Let's raise a glass to making (and bottling) memories together—cheers!

BREWING BASICS

The craft of brewing is ancient, one of the oldest forms of alchemy that we've been dabbling in as a species. There is a theory that the discovery of naturally fermented fruit lying on the ground (and the feelings it gave after consuming it) developed into the purposeful pursuit of alcohol, or that water simply leaked into a honey storage jar and the resulting fermentation was a happy accident that we gleefully recreated.

We've been playing with brewing technology for so long that there are thousands of methods for brewing alcoholic drinks. Many modern brewers prefer a more scientific, measured approach to their craft. They use hydrometers to measure the potential alcohol content and refining agents to help clear their brews, and they create exactly measured recipes that can be easily replicated. There are also wild brewers who pursue a slightly more chaotic path, using wild yeasts or no additives, making an ephemeral brew that can never be exactly repeated.

The methods that I use fall in the middle of those two roads. It is easy to appreciate the use of sanitizers and the convenience of some modern brewing equipment, but you can limit the use of chemical additives in mead, wine, cider and beer and still end up with a tasty brew.

Ultimately, there are as many methods of brewing as there are brewers! Once you get comfortable with the basic techniques, I'll bet you'll find yourself tweaking recipes, skipping ingredients, adding new ones and otherwise making your brews your own. Enjoy the process and do what works best for you.

Seek out your local community of brewers. If you have friends around who like to brew, geek out with them, or see if there is a local homebrew club that you can join. Check for a homebrew supply shop in your area. That's a great way to meet a group of folks who won't get annoyed when you prattle on about your techniques! It will afford you the opportunity to listen and learn from the methods of others. A group to share with will ensure that you'll always be learning new things to try.

WHY ONE-GALLON BATCHES?

Brewing batches of bubbly booze at home is a great hobby, but it can seem a little intimidating when you begin. The initial cost of equipment, ingredients and your time can seem quite steep if you jump straight into 5- and 6-gallon (19- and 23-L) batches.

If cost is not a factor, your own size, strength and physical ability might play into the decision to craft small batches of brew. After a few brewing sessions where I had to heave and haul full 5-gallon (19-L) carboys around on my own, I realized that I should probably explore more manageable fermenting projects for someone of my size and strength. The results of my explorations are the recipes for 1-gallon (3.8-L) brews in this book.

Time is also a commodity for many people. If you have a busy schedule, it's far easier to set aside an hour or two in an evening to brew or bottle a small batch than it is to dedicate half a day to a larger-scale brew project.

Finally, small batches allow you to play mad scientist when it comes to brewing. If you enjoy experimenting with flavors and techniques, smaller batches mean less cost involved in testing out your crazy ideas! Once you have a successful recipe, you can scale it up and re-create it as a bigger brew so that you have plenty of it to enjoy with friends and family. If you want to expand a 1-gallon recipe up to a 5-gallon recipe, you can do it! For most brews, you can simply multiply all ingredients (except the yeast) by five. You would use the whole yeast packet in that case.

If you are worried, take time to do a bit of research. Visit the forums at GotMead.com and WineMakingTalk.com and ask for advice on your recipes. Both sites are great resources with extensive archives and active users. When in doubt, visit your local homebrew shop to seek advice.

SUGGESTED EQUIPMENT FOR BEGINNERS

To get started with making your own brews at home, you will first need to invest in some equipment.

Acquiring a set of homebrew equipment isn't terribly expensive if you gather your supplies bit by bit, over time. Keep an eye on local classified ads, homebrew message boards or your local Freecycle chapter. You can often find wine bottles, beer bottles and sometimes even discounted homebrew equipment from someone who is giving up the hobby! You can also get "free" gallon (3.8-L) jugs by buying local apple cider or gallons of cheap wine and reusing the bottles.

Before you buy new brewing equipment from retailers online, you should check to see if you have a local homebrew supply shop nearby. Try shopping there first, even if it costs a bit more. It is worth it to get to know the staff (and fellow brewers), support a local business and get a deeper understanding of the various supplies by browsing them in person instead of on a screen.

At the bare minimum, you'll need the following supplies:

- Digital scale

- Thermometer

- Brewing pot/stockpot

- Long spoon

- Fermenter (glass jug and brew bucket)

- Bung and airlock

- Sanitizer

- Wine thief/sanitized straw

- Siphon tube/racking cane

- Bottles and caps or corks

- Funnel

- Straining bags and strainer

DIGITAL SCALE

I rely on a gram scale for specialized ingredients, such as dried dandelion root and hops, because it provides the most accurate measurement.

THERMOMETER

A thermometer is handy to have when brewing. The temperature of the must or wort can affect the yeast, sugars and pH levels of your brew. There is a wide range of thermometers available, from analog to digital options, including Bluetooth-enabled thermometers for constant temperature tracking!

BREWING POT/STOCKPOT

A 1-gallon (3.8-L) pot will work for many brews, but you'll need a 2-gallon (7.5-L) pot for the beers. It's best to have a lid that fits it well, as that will reduce boiling time and help to steep the herbs.

LONG SPOON

You'll need a spoon long enough to reach the bottom of your pot so that you can stir sugar, honey or other ingredients into the hot water. Many people prefer a metal or silicone spoon since those are easier to sanitize, but if you want to use only wild yeasts, a wooden spoon can become your magical brewing wand!

FERMENTER

The glass jugs that are used in this book are called carboys, demijohns or fermenters in the brewing process. These are 1-gallon (3.8-L) bottles that apple cider (or cheap wine) is often packaged in. If you get one secondhand, check it over carefully for cracks or chips before using it and discard any jugs that are questionable.

Some recipes need 2-gallon (7.5-L) plastic brew buckets as fermenters. These are great for making brews with fresh fruit, as we'll explore later on, and essential for beers. You can easily drill a hole in the lid to accommodate a rubber gasket and an airlock. Brew shops sell brew buckets with airlock-ready lids and spigots on the side to make things easier at bottling time.

BUNG AND AIRLOCK

The bung is the plug that sits in the mouth of the gallon jug. A #6 or #6.5 bung should fit the mouth of most 1-gallon (3.8-L) jugs. Make sure that you are getting a bung with a hole drilled through it for the airlock. It's also good to have solid bungs on hand—they are good for closing off your jug when you shake up your brew.

The airlock is the plastic part that sits in the bung and serves to release the gases created during fermentation. They keep the brew safe as it ferments. The airlock is filled with liquid that acts as a seal so that the gases can escape and unwanted bacteria and yeasts can't get in.

SANITIZER

I prefer to use an oxygen-based, no-rinse sanitizer like One Step, which you can find at any homebrew supply shop, but you can also use bleach to sanitize your equipment in a pinch. If you use bleach to sanitize, make sure that you are using it correctly (1 tablespoon [15 ml] to 1 gallon [3.8 L] of water) and that your supplies are rinsed very well to prevent residual bleach from killing off your yeasts. Bleach can also cause off-flavors by soaking into the softer plastic equipment, like siphon tubes, so be careful!

WINE THIEF/SANITIZED STRAW

A wine thief is a handy plastic or glass pipette-style tube that you can stick into your primary fermenter to draw out a bit of the liquid. They generally cost under $10 and are easy to find at a homebrew supply shop, but if you don't have one handy, you can use a regular straw or bit of tubing to get your sample of brew. Sanitize the straw or tube and dip it into the fermenting brew. Seal off the other end with your fingertip, pull it out of the jug and transfer the liquid into a small glass so you can give it a taste.

SIPHON TUBE/RACKING CANE

This bit of tubing is very important, as it is used to transfer the brews from one container to another. You can use a few feet of 5/16-inch (8-mm) food-safe rubber tubing and a 24-inch (61-cm) racking cane, but I prefer using an auto-siphon to make things easier—just a few pumps and your bubbly brew will flow. The 3/8-inch (1-cm) or mini auto-siphons are the perfect size for 1-gallon (3.8-L) jugs and 2-gallon (7.5-L) fermenting buckets.

BOTTLES AND CAPS OR CORKS

There are many types of bottles that you can use to store and age your brews. Each type has its strengths and weaknesses.

Swing-top bottles (also known as Grolsch bottles) are my favorite way to store mead, wine or cider. They come in various sizes, shapes and colors. Be sure that any swing-top bottles that you purchase secondhand are intended for food use, as there are thin glass versions sold for crafts that won't stand up to the pressures of fermentation. Swing-top bottles can be reused as long as they are in good shape. Check them over for cracks or chips, and discard a bottle if you find any. As a bonus, you will not require special equipment for bottling since the caps are attached. Gaskets used between the cap and the bottle for swing-top bottles are inexpensive. They can be reused many times, but you should replace them if you see any cracks or chips in the rubber. The number of swing-top bottles you need to bottle a gallon will vary depending on the sizes you have on hand.

Traditional wine bottles with corks are the best choice for any mead, wine or cider that you hope to store for a long time. They are also aesthetically pleasing! You will have to purchase corks and a corker to use this method of bottling. Most 1-gallon (3.8-L) batches will fill 6 standard wine bottles (750 ml, approximately 25.4 ounces).

Beer bottles are for more than just beer! I often use beer bottles for all of my brews, including mead, wine and cider. Be sure to get oxygen-absorbing bottle caps if you intend to use beer bottles for long-term storage of your brews. If you go through craft beer like I do, you'll have plenty of bottles for "free" and replacement caps are inexpensive! You will need to purchase a capper to use this method. Most 1-gallon (3.8-L) batches will fill 8 to 12 beer bottles, depending on size.

FUNNEL

A funnel that fits into the neck of a gallon (3.8-L) jug makes pouring liquids into the carboy much easier. I find that an 8-inch (20-cm) funnel works well with the 1-gallon (3.8-L) jugs, while some of the larger funnels, up to 14 inches (35.5 cm), work well with the larger-mouthed fermenting buckets. Some funnels come with built-in screens, which can be very handy when straining the must!

STRAINING BAGS AND STRAINER

Some people don't mind flower petals or chunks of fruit floating in their ferment, so consider these to be optional.

You can use cheesecloth to tie up herbs that you put in the brew, but when it comes to brewing with large bits of fruit, a straining bag is worth the cost. These nylon bags hold fruit, hops pellets or any other ingredient that would otherwise float in your fermenting brew.

It is also handy to have a colander or metal mesh strainer on hand for straining your wort or must into the carboy.

YEAST AND OTHER INGREDIENTS

The following are the main ingredients in a recipe. You will also add flavoring agents that will be specified in each particular recipe.

WATER

Water is the main ingredient in every brew, so you should be sure that the water you use has a good flavor! The well at my home provides a mineral-rich water that tastes quite nice. If you intend to use treated tap water, it is suggested that you boil it and let it sit for a few hours before using it to allow the chlorine to evaporate. Bottled water is an option, but avoid using distilled water as it has no nutrients to help the fermentation along.

YEAST

The magic ingredient in every brew, whether mead, wine, cider or beer, is yeast! Yeast is a colony of tiny, single-celled fungi that consume sugar and expel carbon dioxide and ethyl alcohol (the bubbles and the booze). There are more than 20 billion cells in 1 gram of yeast.

There are many varieties of yeast in the world, and the flavors and alcohol content of your final product depend on which kind you use. While you can purchase individual strains of yeast to achieve specific results, keep in mind that yeast is everywhere! It lives on the skin of berries, the rinds of citrus and even in the air around us. Wild yeast can produce wild results. Since you don't know what kind you are getting, using wild yeast is unpopular with the more methodical brewers.

The wine, cider and mead recipes in this book use 2.5 grams (1 tsp) of yeast. Most regular paper packets of yeast from a brew shop are 5 grams (2.3 tsp). You can use half a packet for a recipe and store the rest of the yeast in your fridge in an airtight container, to keep moisture out, until your next batch. Use the opened packet within 2 weeks for best results.

While you can technically use bread or baking yeast, its high alcohol tolerance makes for strong brews with no sweetness and brews made with this yeast often develop odd flavors, especially if they are brewed in a warm place.

YEAST NUTRIENT

Yeast consumes sugar to produce delicious alcohol, but sometimes sugar isn't enough to get the job done. Our fungi friends need more food, in the form of yeast nutrient. You can buy bottles of yeast nutrient from a homebrew shop, but I prefer to use raisins and other fruit to provide the needed boost to my booze. Most of the recipes in this book use raisins, but I omit them when there is enough fruit to make their inclusion redundant.

HERBS AND FLOWERS

Be careful! Use only flowers that you are certain are edible and have not been sprayed by animals or weed killers. Search for a foraging guide in your area or research your plants before you consume them. If you aren't fond of foraging for fresh herbs and flowers, you can use dried flowers and herbs in a recipe, but use less, as aromatic oils are stronger in dried herbs. If a recipe calls for a fresh herb but you only have the dried herb, use one-third of what the recipe asks for. For some of the more aromatic herbs, you may wish to use only one-quarter of the fresh ingredient.

TANNINS

Tannins are an optional addition to any brew. They add a bit of sharp bitterness, which can provide a nice complexity to balance a sweet mead and add depth to its flavor.

Think of the acrid taste when you over-steep a cup of black tea—those are tannins. While their flavor profile is bitter, tannins can provide a lovely balance to a brew, especially meads. Wines and ciders tend to have plenty of their own tannins from grape skins and bitter cider apples, and the bitterness in beer is provided by the hops.

Many of my recipes include black tea to add tannins when there isn't another tannic ingredient. You can also rack your brew onto oak chips to achieve the same effect.

THE BASIC BREWING PROCESS

If you have never brewed an alcoholic beverage before, don't despair! This section will provide a quick guide to the basic steps of brewing. The brewing of mead, wine and cider are very similar in technique, while most of the beer recipes have more steps to follow and more ingredients to add. I will go into more specific details about each type of brew in the introductory recipes for each section.

BREWING

Brew day! This is the first step, where you mix the main ingredients, get the must (wine, mead, cider) or wort (beer) into the primary fermenter and pitch the yeast.

WAITING

This is the hardest part of brewing. After you set up your recipe on brew day, you have to let the yeast work its magic. Fermentation can take anywhere from a few weeks to a few months, depending on the type of brew! You'll know that your brew is ready for the next step when the airlock has stopped bubbling, the jug has mostly cleared and there are no more bubbles rising to the surface of the brew.

TASTING

When the brew has cleared, use a wine thief or a sanitized straw to draw out some of the liquid to taste it. Since it is fresh from the jug, the brew will have a strong alcohol flavor or sharp tones to it that will mellow with age. If you are otherwise happy with the flavor and sweetness of the brew, go ahead and bottle it. Otherwise, you can try racking the brew.

RACKING

Racking is the process by which you take the brew out of the primary fermenter and transfer it into a secondary fermenter. This process removes the brew from the sediment, called the lees or trub (dead yeast, hops or other solids), resting on the bottom of the jug in primary and will help it to clear. Racking also gives you the opportunity to adjust the flavor and sweetness of your brew by adding fruit, honey, sugar syrup or flavoring additives, such as oak chips, to the secondary fermenter.

BACKSWEETENING

Since yeast feeds on sugars, adding more sugars to sweeten while racking could wake up dormant yeast and restart fermentation. If you sweeten while racking, wait at least five days before you bottle your brew. That should give you enough time to make sure the yeast has not kicked back into action.

While I don't use this technique myself, many brewers use potassium sorbate to stabilize their brews before adding sugars and bottling. You can add ½ teaspoon of potassium sorbate to a gallon of mead or cider to stop fermentation and then add your sugar or honey syrup to taste 24 hours later. You can find it in any homebrew shop!

BOTTLING

This is the final step in the process, in which you siphon the finished product from the fermenter into bottles for storing the brew. You will know that it is time to bottle mead, wine or cider when the bubbles stop rising from the bottom of the carboy. Another good rule of thumb is to wait until the brew is so clear that you can hold a book behind the jug and read the text through it. It's always important to label your bottles well with the name of the brew and the date of bottling.

It's a bit more complex to know when to bottle beers. Priming sugar added to the finished beer provides just enough sugar for the yeasts to eat, carbonating the beer in the bottle. Also, many beers are dark and will remain rather opaque, so using clarity to determine completion is probably not a good idea. Most beer recipes will include suggestions for timing.

STORING AND DRINKING

Two weeks after you've bottled your brew, give one a try and see how it is! Beers and ciders are best enjoyed within a year, but meads and wines taste much better as they age. Meads and wines can be stored for a very long time—centuries, in fact! The best way to store them is in corked bottles that are laying on their sides. The reason for that is that the liquid in the bottles keeps the cork wet and therefore sealed. Corked bottles that are stored standing up will end up with dried corks, which can lead to infections or oxidization—either way resulting in a nasty brew!

Heavenly Honey Mead

A taste of honey, tasting much sweeter than wine.
—The Beatles

Honey, water, yeast and time. It's amazing how the simplest of combinations can make such a delicious and complex beverage, much-lauded throughout history and a wide variety of cultures around the world!

Mead is best known in our popular culture as the drink of choice for rowdy Viking folk or a golden potion poured into fine goblets in a medieval court, but honey wine appears in Hindu, Chinese and African history as well.

You can continue this timeless trend by making your own batch of mead. Start out with the master recipe for a simple brew so that you can get the basic idea down first. Then you can confidently take it up a notch with more complex recipes like Blueberry Muffin Mead (page 31) or Lemon and Ginger Mead (page 40). Take a stroll around your garden and see what you can add to your own special Wildflower Mead (page 28). A world of flavors awaits you!

IT'S ALL ABOUT THE HONEY

Honey is more than just a scrumptious treat for the senses. It is a medicine, a preserver of food and, throughout history, a gift given to and assumed to come from the gods themselves.

Before we had access to a bounty of processed sugar in our modern era, honey was the main method of satisfying a sweet tooth. Even so, it was hard-won, either wrested from wild bees or taken from hand-tended, cultivated hives. Both of those methods of harvesting honey include a lot of hard labor and certainly a few stings!

Honey is the combined effort of a ton of tiny little workers who gather pollen from more flowers, trees, herbs and grasses than we can conceive of. It is full of the essences of each of those plants, full of the water that the bees consume from streams and rivers and full of the resins from the tree saps on which they sup. Honey is a medicine, a delight—is it any wonder that we call each other "honey" and send newlywed lovers on their honeymoon?

Since honey is made up of flower nectar, pollen and tree resins, the ecosystem from which bees harvest makes a big difference in the flavor, texture and color of the harvested honey, and therefore, the end result of your mead. There are many varietal kinds of honey gathered from hives surrounded by a single, specific plant. Sourwood is a famous honey here in southern Appalachia. Raspberry honey is light and almost fruity, carrot honey is dark and tastes of malt and star thistle honey is sharp and complex in flavor.

Clover honey, orange blossom honey and wildflower honey are the three most popular (and readily available) choices for meadmakers. Raw, local honey is sometimes a bit more expensive, but it is good to support your local beekeepers and to know where the honey comes from.

MASTER RECIPE: BASIC MEAD

You can make a lovely mead with just a few ingredients. This recipe makes a semisweet mead that has a strong taste of honey with a nice balance of tannins and acids to round out the flavor.

>>>><<<<

1 gal (3.8 L) water, divided

½ lemon, chopped

⅛ cup (20 g) raisins, chopped

1 cup (240 ml) strongly brewed black tea

3 lb (1.4 kg) honey

½ packet (2.5 g) Lalvin D-47 yeast

1. **Gather and sanitize equipment:** Gather your ingredients and your supplies. You'll need a 1- or 2-gallon (3.8- or 7.5-L) stockpot, a long spoon, a funnel, a strainer, a gallon (3.8-L) carboy and a bung and airlock. Sanitize all of the brewing equipment and anything else that will come into contact with your brew.

2. **Make the brew:** Heat ⅔ gallon (2.5 L) of the water in the stockpot to just about boiling. Add the lemon, raisins and tea to the water. Give it a stir and remove the pot from the heat. Let that mix steep for about 15 minutes. Stir in the honey until it is completely dissolved. Once the must is well blended, let it sit for another 10 minutes or so to cool.

3. **Funnel and cool:** Use the funnel and strainer to pour the warm must into the gallon (3.8-L) carboy. Top off the carboy with as much of the remaining ⅓ gallon (1.3 L) of water needed for the must to reach the neck of the jug. Seal it with the bung and airlock to keep everything clean. Allow the must to cool for a few hours.

4. **Add the yeast:** When the glass is cool enough that you can touch the jug on the bottom and not feel the heat, or the must reaches 90°F (32°C), you can pitch the yeast. First, cover the mouth of the carboy. Shake the jug for a minute to add oxygen. Sprinkle the yeast into the jug and then recap the carboy with the bung and airlock.

5. **Ferment:** Label the jug with the brew name and date and set it aside somewhere around 60 to 70°F (16 to 21°C) and out of direct sunlight. After a day or so, you should start to see the bubbles appear, and you can revel in the sound of the jug bubbling until it is done with its fermenting magic! Check the airlock and watch how often it bubbles. You can tell the brew is done when the bubbles have stopped and the mead has cleared. This usually takes about 4 to 6 weeks.

(continued)

6.   **Bottle:** Once the mead is cleared it is time to bottle! Sanitize your bottles, racking cane and caps or corks, if you need them. Set the jug on your counter and put the sanitized bottles at a lower level, either in your sink or on the floor. This helps the siphon to work more effectively. Put one end of the siphon tube in a bottle and the racking cane into the jug and try not to disturb the lees at the bottom. Fill the bottles up to the necks and then cap them. Rinse the bottles and label them.

7.   **Age:** Put the bottles away to age for at least 3 weeks before enjoying the fruits of your labor!

8.   **Serving:** When you open your first bottle of mead, pour a little bit into a glass and let it breathe like you would for a dark red wine. Take a taste and see what you think! If you want to change the flavor and sweetness of your mead, you can make it a spritzer (page 139) or add sugar syrup (page 143) to give it a boost.

TIP: "Must" is the name for the juice or honey water of meads or wines before they ferment.

TIP: Frozen and thawed? When you freeze fresh fruit, the ice crystals break down the cell walls in the fruit, releasing more juices to flavor your brew. This is why many mead recipes in this chapter call for first freezing and then thawing the fruit.

LOVELY LEMON BALM MEAD

Also known as "Sweet Melissa," lemon balm is a heart-lifting, aromatic herb from the mint family. If you've ever grown it, then you'll know that it is vigorous and you often have more lemon balm than you know what to do with. Along with teas, cookies, syrups and sugared leaves, you can use up your harvest with a gallon of bright, invigorating mead!

I've tried this mead with both dried and fresh lemon balm, and I must say that the fresh lemon balm wins, hands down. The dried herb is too tannic and bitter.

1 gal (3.8 L) water, divided

½ lemon, chopped

⅛ cup (20 g) raisins, chopped

1 cup (240 ml) strongly brewed black tea

6 cups (150 g) gently packed fresh lemon balm leaves

3 lb (1.4 kg) honey

½ packet (2.5 g) Lalvin D-47 yeast

1. Gather your ingredients and sanitize your supplies. You'll need two 1- or 2-gallon (3.8- or 7.5-L) stockpots (or a stockpot and a 2-gallon [7.5-L] brew bucket), a long spoon, a funnel, a strainer, a gallon (3.8-L) carboy and a bung and airlock.

2. Heat ⅔ gallon (2.5 L) of the water in the stockpot. Add the lemon, raisins and tea to the water. Give it a stir, then remove the pot from the heat.

3. Put the lemon balm leaves in the second pot or brew bucket. Gently massage and crush the leaves with your fingers to release the aromatic oils.

4. Stir the honey into the warm water until it is completely dissolved. Once the must is well blended, pour it over the lemon balm leaves. Cover that pot with a lid or cloth and let it steep for 15 minutes.

5. Use the funnel and strainer to pour the warm must into the gallon carboy. Top it off with as much of the remaining ⅓ gallon (1.3 L) of water needed for the must to reach the neck of the jug. Seal it with the bung and airlock.

6. When the glass is cool enough to handle, pitch the yeast. First, cover the mouth of the carboy. Shake the jug for a minute to add oxygen, sprinkle the yeast into the jug and then recap the carboy with the bung and airlock. Label the jug with the name of the brew and date and set it aside somewhere out of direct sunlight until it is finished fermenting.

TIP: Lemon balm is an herb that is used to help with relaxation and to boost the mood. It also attracts bees and other pollinators to your garden!

7. Once the mead is cleared, go ahead and bottle (page 24) it. If it is too dry for your taste after it has aged in the bottle, use a sugar syrup (page 143, 144 or 147) to boost the flavor and sweetness at serving time!

WILDFLOWER MEAD

There are lovely days in spring and summer when you can open your windows and smell the flowers and herbs blooming outside. Slather on some sunscreen and get out there and gather flowers to make a mead that is completely unique to your yard, garden or favorite foraging spot. I use peony, rose, yarrow, honeysuckle, bee balm, lemon balm, a sprig of rosemary, a few sprigs of lavender, mugwort, red clover, crimson clover and elderflower. If you prefer to use dried flowers and herbs, use only 1 tablespoon (5 g) of each, so the aromatic oils don't overpower the brew.

4 cups (100 g) fresh flowers and herbs

1 gal (3.8 L) water, divided

½ grapefruit, chopped

⅛ cup (20 g) raisins, chopped

1 cup (240 ml) strongly brewed black tea

3 lb (1.4 kg) honey

½ packet (2.5 g) Lalvin D-47 yeast

1. Gather your ingredients and sanitize your supplies. You'll need two 1- or 2-gallon (3.8- or 7.5-L) stockpots (or a stockpot and a 2-gallon [7.5-L] brew bucket), a long spoon, a funnel, a strainer, a gallon (3.8-L) carboy and a bung and airlock.

2. Prepare the flowers by removing the green parts and stems, using just the petals. Gently massage and crush the flowers and herbs with your fingers to release the aromatic oils as you put them into a stockpot. Set it aside. Don't rinse the flowers, as that will remove the delicate pollens and diminish the flavors. They'll be strained well later so any dirt or small bugs will be removed!

3. Heat ⅔ gallon (2.5 L) of the water in the second stockpot to almost boiling. Add the grapefruit, raisins and tea. Stir and remove the pot from the heat.

4. Stir the honey into the water in the stockpot until it is completely dissolved. Once the must is well blended, pour it over the wildflowers. Cover with a lid or cloth and let the mixture steep for 15 minutes.

5. Use the funnel and strainer to pour the warm must into the gallon (3.8-L) carboy. Top it off with as much of the remaining ⅓ gallon (1.3 L) of water needed for the must to reach the neck of the jug. Seal it with the bung and airlock.

6. When the glass is cool enough to handle, pitch the yeast. First, cover the mouth of the carboy. Shake the jug for a minute to add oxygen. Sprinkle the yeast into the jug and then recap the carboy with the bung and airlock. Label the jug with the brew name and date and set it aside somewhere out of direct sunlight until it is finished fermenting.

7. This mead is a vigorous fermenter. Because of all of the plant matter and potential for wild yeasts, I recommend racking it into a secondary fermenter to help the mead clear more quickly and to remove it from the lees. Bottle (page 24) the mead once it is clear and let it age as long as you can—delicious as it may be, it only gets better with time!

BLUEBERRY MUFFIN MEAD

Sweet, tart and a beautiful color—this bilbemel, or blueberry mead, is a crowd-pleaser! If you are using fresh-picked berries, put them in the freezer and then thaw them for brew day. This recipe omits the citrus fruit and the black tea, as the blueberry skins and seeds will add enough bitterness and tartness to the final product.

FOR THE MEAD

1 gal (3.8 L) water, divided

3 lb (1.4 kg) honey

2 lb (910 g) blueberries, frozen and thawed

⅛ cup (20 g) raisins, chopped

½ packet (2.5 g) Lalvin D-47 yeast

FOR RACKING

1 vanilla bean, sliced lengthwise

1 stick cinnamon

TIP: This bilbemel is delightful as a must, tasty at the time of racking and even better at bottling! Aging further improves this mead. You'll reap a reward if you can stand to leave a bottle to age for a few months.

1. Gather your ingredients and sanitize your supplies. You'll need a 1- or 2-gallon (3.8- or 7.5-L) stockpot, a long spoon, a straining bag, a 2-gallon (7.5-L) brew bucket or crock, a gallon (3.8-L) carboy, a racking cane and a bung and airlock.

2. For the mead, heat ⅔ gallon (2.5 L) of the water in the stockpot, but don't let it boil. Remove the pot from the heat. Stir in the honey and then let it sit for another 10 minutes or so to cool.

3. Pour the blueberries and raisins into the straining bag, tie the bag closed and put it into the brew bucket. Use your spoon to gently mash the berries and release their juices.

4. Carefully pour the warm must over the berries in the bucket. Add the remaining ⅓ gallon (1.3 L) of water to the bucket and let the must cool.

5. When the bucket is cool enough to handle, pitch the yeast. First, sprinkle the yeast into the brew bucket and stir it in to add oxygen and mix in the yeast. Put the lid onto the bucket, making sure it is sealed, and then put the airlock in place. Label the bucket with the name of the brew and the date and set it aside somewhere out of direct sunlight until it is finished fermenting.

6. Give the bucket a swish every day for 3 days. This will give the yeast oxygen and help inhibit mold growth on the floating fruit bag.

7. Transfer the liquid to the carboy. Add the vanilla bean and cinnamon stick. Seal the jug with the bung and airlock. Label your brew with name and date.

8. Bottle (page 24) the mead when it has finished fermenting; this will take 2 to 3 weeks.

ROSEMARY AND CLEMENTINE MEAD

Sweet clementines and pungent rosemary are a lovely combination, especially when paired with wildflower honey. The aroma of this mead makes me think of medieval-era embroidered tapestries and the fine gardens of castle grounds.

The light citrus acidity and the sharp rosemary—a classic flavor duo—make a wonderful summer evening tipple, along with some Manchego cheese, ceviche or a fresh salad.

1 gal (3.8 L) water, divided

⅛ tsp fresh minced rosemary

⅛ cup (20 g) raisins, chopped

5 clementines, zested and juiced, divided

3 lb (1.4 kg) honey

½ packet (2.5 g) Lalvin D-47 yeast

1. Gather your ingredients and sanitize your supplies. You'll need a 1- or 2-gallon (3.8- or 7.5-L) stockpot, a long spoon, a funnel, a strainer, a gallon (3.8-L) carboy and a bung and airlock.

2. Heat ⅔ gallon (2.5 L) of the water in the stockpot. Remove the pot from the heat when the water is about to boil and add the rosemary, raisins and clementine zest. Cover the pot with a lid and let the mixture steep for about 10 minutes. Stir in the honey and let the must cool until you can safely pour it.

3. Use the funnel and strainer to transfer the must into the carboy; add the clementine juice. Top off the carboy with as much of the remaining ⅓ gallon (1.3 L) of water needed for the must to reach the neck of the jug. Seal it with the bung and airlock.

4. Pitch the yeast when the glass is cool enough to handle. First, cover the mouth of the carboy. Shake the jug for a minute to add oxygen. Sprinkle the yeast into the jug and then recap the carboy with the bung and airlock. Label the jug with the name of the brew and the date and set it aside somewhere out of direct sunlight until it is finished fermenting. Bottle (page 24) when ready.

RECIPE NOTE: If you want a stronger flavor, rack this mead into a new carboy a few days before bottling. For racking, add sugar syrup (page 143, 144 or 147) made with clementine zest and rosemary.

GOLDEN MEAD

The health and fitness worlds are abuzz with talk about golden milk. The combination of coconut milk, honey, turmeric, ginger and black pepper is all the rage, appearing in fancy cafes as a latte flavor and even as a truffle at fancy chocolate shops. It isn't just a taste-based trend: golden milk is inspired by Ayurvedic medicine and is a tonic meant to help reduce inflammation and pain in sore joints.

Since oil is not easy to get out of brewing equipment, such as racking canes and siphon tubes, I've omitted all things coconut from this recipe. You will also have vivid yellow brewing equipment if you don't immediately clean it after working this brew. Turmeric is a natural dye and it will stain everything if you aren't careful!

1 gal (3.8 L) water, divided

¼ cup (10 g) thinly sliced ginger

⅛ cup (20 g) raisins, chopped

2 tsp (8 g) ground turmeric

1 tsp black pepper

3 lb (1.4 kg) honey

½ packet (2.5 g) Lalvin D-47 yeast

1. Gather your ingredients and sanitize your supplies. You'll need a 1- or 2-gallon (3.8- or 7.5-L) stockpot, a long spoon, a funnel, a strainer, a gallon (3.8-L) carboy, a racking cane and a bung and airlock.

2. Heat ⅔ gallon (2.5 L) of the water in the stockpot along with the ginger and raisins. Remove the pot from the heat when the water is about to boil; add the turmeric and black pepper. Cover the pot with a lid and let it steep for about 15 minutes. Stir in the honey and let the must cool until you can safely pour it.

3. Strain the must into the carboy and add enough of the remaining ⅓ gallon (1.3 L) of water needed for the must to reach the neck of the jug. Seal it with the bung and airlock.

4. When the glass is cool enough to handle, pitch the yeast. First, cover the mouth of the carboy. Shake the jug for a minute to add oxygen. Sprinkle the yeast into the jug and then recap the carboy with the bung and airlock. Label the jug with the name of the brew and the date and set it aside somewhere out of direct sunlight until it is finished fermenting.

5. If the must is hazy, you can always rack it into a sanitized secondary fermenter and let it rest before bottling (page 24).

RECIPE NOTE: The color of this brew is a neon yellow that is quite stunning. The flavors are sharp and spicy, but balanced, with a slightly bitter earthiness from the turmeric. A few months in the bottle does a wonderful job of mellowing out the complex tones. This Golden Mead is smooth and delicious after a year of aging.

ROSE PETAL AND HIBISCUS MEAD

Oh, so delicate, floral and sensual. This honey wine is made magical with the addition of flower petals. The reddish-pink color of this mead is a feast for the eyes and the floral flavors dance across your tongue like a faerie frolic! Enjoy the romance of this glorious beverage fit for a queen.

1 gal (3.8 L) water, divided

½ cup (8 g) dried rose petals

2 tbsp (5 g) dried hibiscus petals

⅛ cup (20 g) raisins, chopped

½ lemon, chopped

3 lb (1.4 kg) honey

½ packet (2.5 g) Lalvin D-47 yeast

RECIPE NOTE: This recipe can end up a bit dry, but I find that can be pleasant with the bright hibiscus tartness and the floral rose petal notes. Even if you prefer a sweeter mead, bottle this one dry, as it ages beautifully. You can always make a simple syrup (page 143, 144 or 147) to add to glasses at serving time. Rose Petal and Hibiscus Mead is also quite nice when paired with a sparkling clear soda to make it a spritzer (page 139).

1. Gather your ingredients and sanitize your supplies. You'll need a small pot with a lid, a 1- or 2-gallon (3.8- or 7.5-L) stockpot, a long spoon, a funnel, a strainer, a gallon (3.8-L) carboy and a bung and airlock.

2. Boil one-quarter (1 quart [950 ml]) of the water in the small pot. Remove it from the heat, add the rose and hibiscus petals and cover the pot with a lid. Set it aside to steep, making a floral tea.

3. Heat half (1½ quarts [1.4 L]) of the remaining water, the raisins and the lemon in the stockpot. Stir the mixture and remove the pot from the heat when the water is about to boil. Stir in the honey until it is completely dissolved. Once the must is well blended, let it sit for another 10 minutes or so to cool.

4. Use the funnel and strainer to pour both the warm must and the floral tea into the gallon carboy. Top off the carboy with as much of the remaining 1½ quarts (1.4 L) water needed for the must to reach the neck of the jug. Seal it with the bung and airlock to keep everything clean.

5. When the glass is cool enough to handle, pitch the yeast. First, cover the mouth of the carboy. Shake the jug for a minute to add oxygen. Sprinkle the yeast into the jug and then recap the carboy with the bung and airlock. Label the jug with the name of the brew and the date and set it aside somewhere out of direct sunlight until it is finished fermenting. Bottle (page 24) your brew when ready.

TIP: Dried flowers and herbs are often stronger than their fresh counterparts. As the moisture evaporates during the drying process, the aromatic oils within the plant consolidate.

VANILLA BEAN AND CHAMOMILE MEAD

The combination of honey, chamomile and vanilla bean is truly delightful. The honey has the effect of blending the bitter apple flavors from the chamomile and the rich aroma of the vanilla bean to make a golden nectar that calms the heart and soothes the soul.

1 gal (3.8 L) water, divided

½ cup (10 g) dried chamomile

½ orange, zested and juiced

⅛ cup (20 g) raisins, chopped

1 cup (240 ml) strongly brewed black tea

3 lb (1.4 kg) honey

1 vanilla bean, sliced lengthwise

½ packet (2.5 g) Lalvin D-47 yeast

1. Gather your ingredients and sanitize your supplies. You'll need a 1- or 2-gallon (3.8- or 7.5-L) stockpot, a long spoon, a funnel, a strainer, a gallon (3.8-L) carboy and a bung and airlock.

2. Heat ⅔ gallon (2.5 L) of the water in the stockpot. When the water is about to boil, remove it from the heat and add the chamomile, orange zest and juice, raisins and tea to the water. Give it a stir and cover the pot. Let it steep for about 15 minutes.

3. Next, add the honey and stir until it is completely dissolved. Once the must is well blended, let it sit for another 10 minutes or so to cool.

4. Put the vanilla bean in the carboy.

5. Use the funnel and strainer to pour the warm must into the carboy. Add as much of the remaining ⅓ gallon (1.3 L) of water needed for the must to reach the neck of the jug. Seal it with the bung and airlock.

6. When the glass is cool enough to handle, pitch the yeast. First, cover the mouth of the carboy. Shake the jug for a minute to add oxygen. Sprinkle the yeast into the jug and then recap the carboy with the bung and airlock. Label the jug with the name of the brew and the date and set it aside somewhere out of direct sunlight until it is finished fermenting.

7. Bottle (page 24) the mead once it has cleared. Try to wait a few months before tasting it again, because the vanilla deepens over time and the chamomile bitters mellow to produce a rich mead with a complex profile. The longer you age it, the nicer it becomes!

LEMON AND GINGER MEAD

Lemon, ginger and honey are a classic combination! You often hear it suggested as a hot tea to help with a cold or flu. In this mead, the spicy ginger and tart lemon are carried by the sweet honey, making a brew that is equally delicious cold or warmed in a mug on a chilly night.

1 gal (3.8 L) water, divided

1 lemon, zested and juiced, divided

⅛ cup (20 g) raisins, chopped

3½ oz (100 g) fresh ginger, grated

1 cup (240 ml) strongly brewed black tea

3 lb (1.4 kg) honey

½ packet (2.5 g) Lalvin 71B yeast

1. Gather your ingredients and sanitize your supplies. You'll need a 1- or 2-gallon (3.8- or 7.5-L) stockpot, a long spoon, a funnel, a strainer, a gallon (3.8-L) carboy and a bung and airlock.

2. Heat ⅔ gallon (2.5 L) of the water in the stockpot. Add the lemon zest, raisins, ginger and tea to the water. Allow this mix to simmer for about 15 minutes, and then give it a stir and remove the pot from the heat.

3. Stir the honey into the stockpot until it is completely dissolved. Once the must is well blended, let it sit for another 10 minutes or so to cool.

4. Use the funnel and strainer to pour the warm must into the carboy. Add the lemon juice and enough of the remaining ⅓ gallon (1.3 L) of water for the must to reach the neck of the jug. Seal it with the bung and airlock.

5. When the glass is cool enough to handle, pitch the yeast. First, cover the mouth of the carboy. Shake the jug for a minute to add oxygen. Sprinkle the yeast into the jug and then recap the carboy with the bung and airlock. Label the jug with the name of the brew and the date and set it aside somewhere out of direct sunlight until it is finished fermenting.

6. Once the mead has cleared, taste it with a wine thief or sanitized straw. Go ahead and bottle (page 24) it if you like it dry. Otherwise, add ½ cup (120 ml) of sugar syrup (page 143, 144 or 147) to a secondary fermenter and rack the mead on top of it. After a few weeks, that little bit of sweetness will brighten the flavors perfectly!

7. This brew is enjoyable even when it is young, but aging serves it well.

TIP: If you can't find a dark place to leave your jugs while they ferment, put a small shirt or towel around the carboys to shield them from sunlight.

BLACK CHERRY MEAD

This is a dark twist on a golden beverage. Black cherry juice lends a beautiful hue and a deep, tart flavor to the sweet honey mead, making it a lovely drink for autumn nights. Try it mulled (page 140) or garnished with a twist of citrus!

Make sure that the black cherry juice that you buy does not have added preservatives or sugar. Check the label! Citric acid is safe, but if the ingredients list mentions any sulfites, that juice won't work for your brew.

1 gal (3.8 L) water, divided

⅛ cup (20 g) raisins, chopped

1 cup (240 ml) strongly brewed black tea

3 lb (1.4 kg) honey

4½ cups (1 L) black cherry juice

½ packet (2.5 g) Lalvin D-47 yeast

1. Gather your ingredients and sanitize your supplies. You'll need a 1- or 2-gallon (3.8- or 7.5-L) stockpot, a long spoon, a funnel, a strainer, a gallon (3.8-L) carboy and a bung and airlock.

2. Heat ⅔ gallon (2.5 L) of the water in the stockpot. Once the water is about to boil, remove it from the heat. Add the raisins and tea. Let that steep for about 15 minutes, then stir in the honey. Once the must is well blended, let it sit for another 10 minutes or so to cool.

3. Use the funnel to pour the black cherry juice into the carboy and then use the strainer to pour the warm must in. Top off the carboy with as much of the remaining ⅓ gallon (1.3 L) of water needed for the must to reach the neck of the jug. Seal it with the bung and airlock.

4. When the glass is cool enough to handle, pitch the yeast. First, cover the mouth of the carboy. Shake the jug for a minute to add oxygen. Sprinkle the yeast into the jug and then recap the carboy with the bung and airlock. Label the jug with the name of the brew and the date and set it aside somewhere out of direct sunlight until it is finished fermenting. If this brew is hazy, you can always rack it into a sanitized secondary fermenter and let it rest before bottling (page 24).

5. As to be expected, age does this garnet-hued mead well, although it is delicious even at bottling!

HONEYMOON MEAD

It is a common belief that the word honeymoon comes from a time where a newly married couple would be given a month's worth of mead to boost their health and fertility and to bless their new family. This recipe takes that idea even further with the addition of aphrodisiac herbs, including woody, fragrant damiana, rich, sensual vanilla and spicy, hot cinnamon.

1 gal (3.8 L) water, divided

1 stick cinnamon

2 whole cloves

⅛ cup (20 g) raisins, chopped

⅔ cup (16 g) dried damiana

½ lemon, chopped

3 lb (1.4 kg) honey

1 vanilla bean, sliced lengthwise

½ packet (2.5 g) Lalvin D-47 yeast

1. Gather your ingredients and sanitize your supplies. You'll need a 1- or 2-gallon (3.8- or 7.5-L) stockpot, a long spoon, a funnel, a strainer, a gallon (3.8-L) carboy and a bung and airlock.

2. Heat ⅔ gallon (2.5 L) of the water in the stockpot along with the cinnamon stick and cloves. Remove the pot from the heat when the water is about to boil, and add the raisins, damiana and lemon. Cover with a lid and let the mixture steep for about 15 minutes. Stir in the honey and let the must cool until you can safely pour it.

3. Put the vanilla bean in the carboy. Use the funnel and strainer to pour the must into the carboy. Add enough of the remaining ⅓ gallon (1.3 L) of water needed for the must to reach the neck of the jug. Seal it with the bung and airlock.

4. When the glass is cool enough to handle, pitch the yeast. First, cover the mouth of the carboy. Shake the jug for a minute to add oxygen. Sprinkle the yeast into the jug and then recap the carboy with the bung and airlock. Label the jug with the name of the brew and the date and set it aside somewhere out of direct sunlight until it is finished fermenting. If the brew is hazy, you can always rack it into a sanitized secondary fermenter and let it rest before bottling (page 24).

5. When you taste this one at bottling, it is likely that the young brew will be hot and the damiana overpowering, but don't worry. Age mellows this mead into a beautifully spiced brew to be shared with the ones you love!

CYSER (APPLE MEAD)

Oh, this is a dangerously delicious drink! A cyser blurs the lines between the various types of brews, as it is a cross between a mead and a cider. The sweet and highly alcoholic cyser is a hangover waiting to happen if you overindulge! If it is too cloying for your taste, try adding some club soda to give it a bit of sparkle.

Avoid apple juices that are made from concentrate or that contain preservatives. A gallon (3.8 L) jug of fresh, unfiltered cider from a local orchard is ideal!

1 gal (3.8 L) unfiltered apple juice, divided

⅛ cup (20 g) raisins, chopped

2½ lb (1.13 kg) honey

½ packet (2.5 g) Lalvin D-47 yeast

1. Gather your ingredients and sanitize your supplies. You'll need a 1- or 2-gallon (3.8- or 7.5-L) stockpot, a long spoon, a funnel, a strainer, a gallon (3.8-L) carboy and a bung and airlock.

2. Gently heat ½ gallon (1.9 L) of the apple juice and the raisins in the stockpot over medium-low heat. Don't let the juice boil, as that will release the pectin and give you a hazy brew.

3. Heat the juice for a few minutes, until it reaches about 90°F (32°C), then stir in the honey. Remove the pot from the heat and let the mixture steep and cool for about 15 minutes.

4. Use the funnel and strainer to pour the honey-sweetened juice into the carboy. Top it off with as much of the remaining ½ gallon (1.9 L) of juice needed for the must to reach the neck of the jug. The must should be cool enough for you to pitch the yeast immediately.

5. Pitch the yeast. First, cover the mouth of the carboy. Shake the jug for a minute to add oxygen. Sprinkle the yeast into the jug and then recap the carboy with the bung and airlock. Label the jug with the name of the brew and the date, and set it aside somewhere out of direct sunlight until it is finished fermenting.

6. After a few weeks, or when the bubbles stop appearing and the cyser has cleared, go ahead and bottle it (page 24). Cyser is delicious to drink even when it is young, but age does wonders for this heady and potent brew.

PYMENT (GRAPE MEAD)

Another crossover brew—this time, honey meets grape juice in a combination called pyment.
This is a very sweet mead with a potent grape flavor.

FOR THE MEAD

1 gal (3.8 L) grape juice, white or red, divided

2 lb (910 g) honey

½ packet (2.5 g) Lalvin D-47 yeast

FOR RACKING

5 g lightly toasted oak chips

½ cup (120 ml) rum, brandy or whiskey (or enough to cover the chips)

1. Gather your ingredients and sanitize your supplies. You'll need a 1- or 2-gallon (3.8- or 7.5-L) stockpot, a long spoon, a funnel, a gallon (3.8-L) carboy and a bung and airlock.

2. For the mead, gently heat ½ gallon (1.9 L) of the grape juice in the stockpot over medium-low heat. When the juice reaches 90°F (32°C), stir in the honey. Remove the pot from the heat and let the mixture steep and cool for about 15 minutes.

3. Use the funnel to pour the honey-sweetened juice into the carboy. Top it off with as much of the remaining ½ gallon (1.9 L) of juice needed for the must to reach the neck of the jug. The must should be cool enough for you to pitch the yeast immediately.

4. Pitch the yeast. First, cover the mouth of the carboy. Shake the jug for a minute to add oxygen. Sprinkle the yeast into the jug and then recap the carboy with the bung and airlock. Label the jug with the name of the brew and the date and set it aside somewhere out of direct sunlight until it is finished fermenting.

5. A day before racking your pyment over to a secondary fermenter, sanitize a jar. Put the oak chips in the jar and pour your booze of choice over them. Some of the chips will float, but that is fine. Put a lid on the jar and let it sit overnight. Sanitize the first carboy.

6. On racking day, put the boozy oak chips in the carboy, then rack the pyment over on top of them. Seal the carboy with the bung and airlock. The oak chips lend tannic flavor to your brew to give it more balance.

7. After fermentation has stopped, give the pyment a taste. If you are happy with it, go ahead and bottle (page 24) it. If you'd rather something sweeter, rack it onto Ginger-Honey Syrup (page 144) and give it a bit more time in the jug to make sure that fermentation does not start up again. Bottle (page 24) when ready.

Fruit and Country Wines

Either give me more wine or leave me alone.

—Rumi

Wine has a heady reputation. This ancient brew has enchanted the senses of mortals for thousands of years. It loosens tongues, making it the drink of poets and madmen. It makes even the stodgiest people feel luxurious and sensual. What could be more romantic than a glass of wine shared between lovers?

The buzz from fermented grapes and herbs has been woven into the tapestry of human history—join in with your own wild wines! You can make wine from fresh fruit (foot-crushing not required), from fruit juice or even from a tea or herbal infusion. Dive in and try your own take on Concord Wine (page 53), Grapefruit Wine (page 69) or the unique Scarborough Fair Wine (page 70) made with culinary herbs.

LET'S DEFINE "WINE"

The world of wine is a many varied one. There are dedicated wine drinkers in every country and in every class. For as many bottles as there are of fine, rare wine aging in dusty cellars, there are also as many jugs of sweet strawberry wine lighting up country nights.

We've been stomping grapes and fermenting the juice into heady beverages used in celebration and exultation for centuries, so it's no surprise that grapes are usually the first thing that comes to people's minds when you mention wine.

Wine varietals are made from very specific strains of grapes. Shiraz, Malbec, Cabernet, Riesling, Chardonnay, Gewürztraminer—each of these wines are named after the grapes that are used to make them. But what about the world of wine beyond the vine?

Country wines, or hedgerow wines, are made from an abundant harvest of fruit, vegetables or herbs. Making wine is the perfect thing to do with a glut of peaches, strawberries, blackberries or any other sweet treat growing in your garden. If you are brave, you can even find recipes for tomato, potato or corncob wine!

You can make herbal wines from aromatic plants, common culinary herbs or from edible flowers. Consider the honeysuckle, rose or elderflower—their ephemeral scents can translate into a delightful wine that dances on the palate.

What is it that allows all of these varied fermented beverages to be defined as wine? It comes down to what it is that is being fermented. In the last chapter, the main fermentable sugar used was honey, but all of the recipes in this chapter are wines, because they are made with granulated sugar.

MASTER RECIPE: FRUIT WINE

This wine is made using one of the simplest recipes possible. All you need is juice, sugar and yeast.

For this version, I reconstitute three cans of frozen Concord grape juice concentrate, but you can use any bottled or frozen grape juice that does not contain preservatives or added sugars.

A warning: this tends to be a very aggressive, bubbling ferment! You may want to put your carboy in a place where you don't mind sticky, sweet fruit juice seeping out of the airlock. You can set your vigorously fermenting jugs on a towel in the bathtub with the shower curtain closed overnight, or in a plastic storage bin if you have one large enough. If the airlock gets filled with bubbles and wine, simply clean it, sanitize it and replace it until the fermentation calms down.

1 gal (3.8 L) grape juice, divided

1 cup (200 g) sugar

½ packet (2.5 g) Lalvin K1-V116 yeast

1. **Gather and sanitize equipment:** Gather your ingredients and sanitize your supplies. You'll need a gallon (3.8-L) carboy, a funnel and a bung and airlock.

2. **Make the brew:** Pour ½ gallon (1.9 L) of the grape juice into the carboy. Add the sugar to the remaining ½ gallon (1.9 L) juice in the original bottle, close it and shake it until the sugar is completely dissolved.

3. **Funnel:** Use the funnel to pour the sweetened juice into the carboy with the plain juice. If necessary, top off the carboy with water until the must reaches the neck of the jug.

4. **Add the yeast:** Pour in the yeast and cover the mouth of the carboy with a solid bung or with a clean hand. Shake the jug for a minute or two to mix in the yeast and add oxygen, and then recap the carboy with the bung and airlock.

5. **Ferment:** Label the jug with the brew name and date and set it aside somewhere around 60 to 70°F (16 to 21°C) and out of direct sunlight. After a day or so you should start to see the bubbles appear and you can revel in the sound of the jug bubbling until it is done with its fermenting magic! As with the meads, simply check the airlock and watch how often it bubbles. You can tell fermentation is done when the bubbles have stopped and the wine has cleared. This usually takes about 4 to 6 weeks. Taste the wine again after that week or two and see how things are progressing. If the fermentation appears to be over and you are happy with the flavor, go ahead and bottle your wine. If it isn't sweet enough, consider adding sugar syrup (page 143) or making a spritzer (page 139) when you serve it!

6. **Taste:** Give your wine a taste with a wine thief or sanitized straw when you think it is done. It will probably be dry, as many of the sugars are eaten away during the busy fermentation. If that suits your palate, skip to step 8, bottling. For a sweeter wine, proceed to step 7.

7. **Rack, if desired:** If you want a sweeter flavor, rack the wine to another sanitized jug with 1 cup (240 ml) of sugar syrup (page 143, 144 or 147) in the bottom of it. Put in a new bung and airlock and set aside the wine for another week or two, just in case fermentation restarts.

> **TIP:** If you want to stop fermentation completely before adding sugars and back sweetening your wine, look into using potassium sorbate. This additive ceases the yeast's activity and lets you sweeten without the threat of fermentation starting again.

8. **Bottle:** Once you are happy with the flavor, it is time to bottle! Sanitize your bottles, racking cane and caps or corks, if you need them. Set the jug on your counter and put the sanitized bottles at a lower level, either in your sink or on the floor. This helps the siphon to work more effectively. Put one end of the siphon tube in a bottle and the racking cane into the jug and try not to disturb the lees at the bottom. Fill the bottles up to the necks and then cap them. Rinse and label the bottles.

9. **Age:** Put the bottles away, in a cool environment out of direct sunlight, to age for at least a few weeks before enjoying the fruits of your labor!

> **RECIPE NOTES:** If you use frozen grape juice concentrate, reconstitute the juice in a large pitcher, following the instructions on the label. Add the sugar to the pitcher and stir until the sugar is completely dissolved. Then, transfer the sweetened mixture to the carboy.
>
> When I say "sugar," I mean cane sugar. For a "clean" flavor, use white granulated sugar. For a richer flavor reminiscent of rum or caramel, use brown sugar, turbinado, demerara or piloncillo.

SPICED POMEGRANATE WINE

Be still my heart! Here's a wine made with bottled fruit juice, but this is a much more complex creation. This pomegranate wine has a rich, deep flavor. It is reminiscent of a Beaujolais, with a touch of sweetness that lingers on the tongue.

The spices in the recipe do not live at the forefront, but contribute to a balanced base for the tart pomegranate to rest upon. This wine is an excellent companion to warm you on cold winter days, especially when mulled (page 140)!

3 cups (720 ml) water, plus more if needed

20 grains of paradise or 5 black peppercorns, crushed

2 star anise, crushed

1 stick cinnamon

12 cardamom seeds, crushed

⅛ cup (20 g) raisins, chopped

½ orange, chopped

2 lb (910 g) sugar

2 qt (1.9 L) pomegranate juice

½ packet (2.5 g) Lalvin K1-V116

TIP: Drink Spiced Pomegranate Wine from a crystal goblet if you have one—this scarlet wine with a rich bouquet is best served in a decadent fashion!

1. Gather your ingredients and sanitize your supplies. You'll need a 1- or 2-gallon (3.8- or 7.5-L) stockpot, a long spoon, a funnel, a strainer, a gallon (3.8-L) carboy and a bung and airlock.

2. Boil the water in the stockpot along with the grains of paradise, star anise, cinnamon, cardamom seeds, raisins and orange. Let it simmer for about 20 minutes and then remove it from the heat. Add the sugar to the pot and stir it well until it is completely dissolved.

3. Use the funnel and strainer to transfer the spiced sugar water into the carboy. Add the pomegranate juice to the jug. If there is space left, top off the carboy with water until the must reaches the neck of the jug. Seal it with the bung and airlock to keep everything clean.

4. When the glass is cool enough to handle, pitch the yeast. First, cover the mouth of the carboy. Shake the jug for a minute to add oxygen. Sprinkle the yeast into the jug and then recap the carboy with the bung and airlock. Label the jug with the name of the brew and the date and set it aside somewhere out of direct sunlight until it is finished fermenting. Bottle (page 54) when ready.

RECIPE NOTE: This wine is hazy and thick, but racking it to secondary for a while helps it to clear a bit before bottling.

PINEAPPLE WINE

Pineapple is one of my favorite fruits because it is tart, sweet and so juicy! It's easy to imagine it being a tasty brew, but pineapple wine can be very finicky. The acidic flavors can become hot and metallic tasting after the wine is fermented. I brewed a couple of batches of rocket fuel before I finally found a method that worked.

Don't make this wine with the thin, bright yellow pineapple juice that you find in the metal tins at the grocer. You'll get nicer results from a juice of pineapple blended with other fruit, which will give you a more full-bodied, sweet wine. Check the ingredients label to make sure that there are no preservatives!

2 qt (1.9 L) water, divided

⅛ cup (20 g) raisins, chopped

1 lb (455 g) sugar

1 cup (240 ml) strongly brewed black tea

2 qt (1.9 L) pineapple and pear fruit juice blend

½ packet (2.5 g) Lalvin K1-V116 yeast

1. Gather your ingredients and sanitize your supplies. You'll need a 1- or 2-gallon (3.8- or 7.5-L) stockpot, a long spoon, a funnel, a strainer, a gallon (3.8-L) carboy and a bung and airlock.

2. Heat 1 quart (0.95 L) of the water in the stockpot until it comes to a boil. Remove the pot from the heat and stir in the raisins, sugar and tea. Stir until the sugar is completely dissolved. Let the mixture cool until you can safely pour it.

3. Use the funnel and strainer to strain the must into the carboy. Strain in the fruit juice blend. Top off the jug with as much of the remaining quart (0.95 L) of water needed for the must to reach the neck. Seal it with the bung and airlock.

4. When the glass is cool enough to handle, pitch the yeast. First, cover the mouth of the carboy. Shake the jug for a minute to add oxygen. Sprinkle the yeast into the jug and then recap the carboy with the bung and airlock. Label the jug with the name of the brew and the date and set it aside somewhere out of direct sunlight until it is finished fermenting.

5. This wine is a vigorous fermenter! Keep the carboy in an easy-to-clean spot for the first few nights, just in case wine bubbles foam out of the airlock.

6. Consider racking this wine onto a cup of sugar syrup (page 143, 144 or 147) in a sanitized secondary carboy. This will brighten the flavor after such an active fermentation. Before proceeding to bottle, let the secondary carboy rest for a week after racking to make sure that fermentation hasn't restarted.

7. The more pulp there was in the juice, the harder it is to get this wine to clear. Be patient—good things come to those who wait. Bottle (page 54) when ready.

HONEYSUCKLE WINE

Ah, sweet honeysuckle! It brings back memories of lying on your back in the sunshine, sipping the nectar from the white and yellow flowers like a lazy honeybee.

Honeysuckle is an invasive plant that grows almost everywhere, so it should be easy to find in your area. Forage the fresh, white flowers on the day you will use them, or the unmistakable flavor of wilting flowers will fill your wine jug.

This wine is so light and sweet, and the honey nectar so strong, that many of my taste-testers thought that it was a mead. The aroma of the honeysuckle is a joy in your glass, whether dry or brightened with a bit of syrup (page 143, 144 or 147) to make it sweet!

6 cups (72 g) fresh honeysuckle flowers

¼ cup (40 g) golden raisins, chopped

1 gal (3.8 L) water, divided

2 lb (910 g) sugar

½ packet (2.5 g) Lalvin 71B yeast

1. Gather your ingredients and sanitize your supplies. You'll need two 1- or 2-gallon (3.8- or 7.5-L) stockpots, a long spoon, a funnel, a strainer, a gallon (3.8-L) carboy and a bung and airlock.

2. Prepare your flowers after picking them by pinching off the sepal, or the green bits at the end of the petals. Don't rinse your flowers or the delicate pollen will be lost—instead, we'll strain the flowers before we put them into the jug.

3. Place the flowers and the raisins in one pot and set it aside. Fill the other pot with ⅔ gallon (2.5 L) of the water and bring it to a boil. Remove the pot from the heat and stir in the sugar until it is completely dissolved.

4. Pour the hot, syrupy water over the flowers and raisins, put a lid on and let the mixture steep for 30 minutes. Let the must cool until you can safely pour it.

5. Use the funnel and strainer to pour the must into the carboy. Add as much of the remaining ⅓ gallon (1.3 L) of water needed for the must to reach the neck of the carboy. Seal it with the bung and airlock to keep everything clean.

6. When the jug is cool enough to handle, pitch the yeast. First, cover the mouth of the carboy. Shake the jug for a minute to add oxygen. Sprinkle the yeast into the jug and then recap the carboy with the bung and airlock. Label the jug with the name of the brew and the date and set it aside somewhere out of direct sunlight until it is finished fermenting. Bottle (page 54) when ready.

PEPPERMINT WINE

Mint wine? Oh, yes! This herbal tea-based wine is an experience unto itself. It cleanses the palate with a hint of minty notes, and it also relieves stomach discomfort, making it ideal to serve between courses in a big meal or as an after-dinner drink.

I've provided instructions for both fresh and dried mint. The flavors achieved with the fresh mint are subtler than the dried mint, but either will do the trick. If you have a vigorous mint plant, finding 4 cups (48 g) of fresh leaves is easy to do! Try this with apple mint or chocolate mint for a nice variation.

1 gal (3.8 L) water, divided

½ lemon, chopped

¼ cup (80 g) raisins, chopped

2 lb (910 g) sugar

4 cups (48 g) lightly packed fresh mint leaves, or 30 g dried mint

½ packet (2.5 g) Lalvin D-47 yeast

1.   Gather your ingredients and sanitize your supplies. You'll need a 1- or 2-gallon (3.8- or 7.5-L) stockpot, a long spoon, a funnel, a strainer, a gallon (3.8-L) carboy and a bung and airlock.

2.   Heat ⅔ gallon (2.5 L) of the water in the stockpot until it comes to a boil. Remove it from the heat and stir in the lemon, raisins, sugar and mint. Cover the pot with a lid and let the mixture steep for about 10 minutes. Let the must cool until you can safely pour it.

3.   Use the funnel and strainer to pour the must into the carboy. Top it off with as much of the remaining ⅓ gallon (1.3 L) of water needed for the must to reach the neck of the jug. Seal it with the bung and airlock.

4.   When the glass is cool enough to handle, pitch the yeast. First, cover the mouth of the carboy. Shake the jug for a minute to add oxygen. Sprinkle the yeast into the jug and then recap the carboy with the bung and airlock. Label the jug with the name of the brew and the date and set it aside somewhere out of direct sunlight until it is finished fermenting. Bottle (page 54) when ready.

TIP: A dry mint wine is tasty when served with summer meals, especially a fruit bar and other cold foods. Add a bit of sparkling water (page 139) to brighten the mint flavors and make a nice after-dinner spritzer.

RECIPE NOTE: This is one of those brews that needs a bit of age. Wait at least 6 months before tasting your first bottle, then see what you think of this unique brew!

ELDERBERRY AND ROSE HIP WINE

Wild elderberries dot the fields and hedgerows of North America and much of Europe.
The dark purple berries that form in summer are not tasty when eaten fresh off the branch,
but when cooked down, they impart a rich and tart flavor and color to brews, syrups, desserts
and even medicines. Elderberry is used in herbal medicine to treat symptoms of severe colds and
flu, and rose hips are a natural source of vitamin C, so this is good for you . . . right?

1 gal (3.8 L) water, divided

1 cup (60 g) dried elderberries

1 tbsp (10 g) dried rose hips

½ lemon, chopped

⅛ cup (20 g) raisins, chopped

1 stick cinnamon

.08 oz (2 g) fresh ginger, thinly sliced

2 lb (910 g) sugar

½ packet (2.5 g) Lalvin K1-V116 yeast

1.   Gather your ingredients and sanitize your supplies. You'll need a 1- or 2-gallon (3.8- or 7.5-L) stockpot, a long spoon, a funnel, a strainer, a gallon (3.8-L) carboy and a bung and airlock.

2.   Heat ⅔ gallon (2.5 L) of the water in the stockpot with the elderberries, rose hips, lemon, raisins, cinnamon and ginger. Let it simmer for 10 minutes and remove it from the heat. Cover the pot with a lid and let the mixture steep for about 10 minutes. Stir in the sugar until it is completely dissolved. Let the must cool until you can safely pour it.

3.   Use the funnel and strainer to transfer the must into the carboy. Top it off with as much of the remaining ⅓ gallon (1.3 L) of water needed for the must to reach the neck of the jug. Seal it with the bung and airlock.

4.   When the jug is cool enough to handle, pitch the yeast. First, cover the mouth of the carboy. Shake the jug for a minute to add oxygen. Sprinkle the yeast into the jug and then recap the carboy with the bung and airlock. Label the jug with the name of the brew and the date and set it aside somewhere out of direct sunlight until it is finished fermenting. Bottle (page 54) when ready.

TIP: This sweet, tart brew has a lovely color that matches the berry and citrus flavor. Try mulling this brew for a cold-weather treat (page 140)!

STRAWBERRY AND LINDEN FLOWER WINE

Strawberry wine is always a crowd-pleaser, because it's so bright in color and flavor, and reminiscent of the warm days of early summer. The vanilla bean adds depth and smooths out the acidity of the berries, while the linden flowers and their light vanilla aroma are just icing on the cake!

FOR THE WINE
1 gal (3.8 L) water, divided

⅛ cup (20 g) raisins, chopped

½ lemon, chopped

½ cup (10 g) dried linden flowers

2 lb (910 g) sugar

3 lb (1.4 kg) fresh strawberries, frozen and then thawed

½ packet (2.5 g) Lalvin K1-V116 yeast

FOR RACKING
1 vanilla bean, sliced lengthwise

TIP: Linden is also known as "basswood" in the American South. It is a tree that attracts bees and other pollinators with its lovely white flowers.

1.   Gather your ingredients and sanitize your supplies. You'll need a 1- or 2-gallon (3.8- or 7.5-L) stockpot, a long spoon, a straining bag, a 2-gallon (7.5-L) brew bucket, a funnel, a strainer, a gallon (3.8-L) carboy, a racking cane and a bung and airlock.

2.   Heat ⅔ gallon (2.5 L) of the water in the stockpot with the raisins and lemon until almost boiling. Remove it from the heat and stir in the linden flowers. Cover the pot with a lid and let the mixture steep for about 10 minutes. Stir in the sugar until it is completely dissolved.

3.   Put the thawed strawberries in a straining bag and tie it shut. Place it in the bottom of the bucket and gently mash it with your spoon.

4.   When the must in the stockpot is cool enough to handle, strain it into the bucket and stir it. Add the remaining ⅓ gallon (1.3 L) of water. Seal the bucket with the airlock.

5.   When the brew bucket is cool enough to handle, pitch the yeast. First, sprinkle the yeast into the brew bucket and stir it in to add oxygen and mix in the yeast. Put the lid onto the bucket, making sure it is sealed, and then put the airlock in place. Label the bucket with the name of the brew and the date and set it aside somewhere out of direct sunlight for 3 to 4 days. Pick up the bucket and give it a gentle swish every day to help keep it mixed and to inhibit mold growth on the surface of the wine.

6.   For racking, place the vanilla bean in the carboy. You also have an opportunity to add sugar syrup (page 143, 144 or 147) if you want a sweeter brew. Rack your wine from the bucket into the carboy. Seal it with the bung and airlock and let it work until you no longer see bubbles. Bottle (page 54) when ready.

GRAPEFRUIT WINE

My grapefruit wine is made with fresh fruit. It is a labor-intensive process, but it yields a bright, complex wine with the lovely trademark bitterness and sourness that you expect from a fresh grapefruit. This wine has a definite grapefruit aroma and a subtle citrus flavor. It leaves a pithy, bitter taste on the back of the tongue. Try one after a month in the bottle, and you might be pleasantly surprised at how mellow it has become!

6 grapefruits

¼ cup (40 g) raisins, chopped

1 gal (3.8 L) water, divided

2 lb (910 g) sugar

½ packet (2.5 g) Lalvin 71B yeast

1. Gather your ingredients and sanitize your supplies. You'll need a straining bag, a 2-gallon (7.5-L) brew bucket, a long spoon, a 1- or 2-gallon (3.8- or 7.5-L) stockpot, a funnel, a strainer, a gallon (3.8-L) carboy, a racking cane and a bung and airlock.

2. Zest 2 of the grapefruits, removing as much of the white pith as possible, and put the zest in the straining bag. Peel the remaining 4 grapefruits. Segment all the grapefruits and place the segments in the straining bag. Add the raisins, then tie the bag shut and place it in the brew bucket. Gently mash the fruit with the spoon to release the juices.

3. Heat ⅔ gallon (2.5 L) of the water in the stockpot until it comes to a boil. Remove the pot from the heat and stir in the sugar until it is completely dissolved. Let it cool for about 10 minutes.

4. Strain the hot sugar water into the brew bucket and stir it well. Add the remaining ⅓ gallon (1.3 L) of water.

5. When the brew bucket is cool enough to handle, pitch the yeast. First, sprinkle the yeast into the brew bucket and stir it in to add oxygen and mix in the yeast. Put the lid onto the bucket, making sure it is sealed, and then put the airlock in place. Label the bucket with the name of the brew and the date and set it aside somewhere out of direct sunlight for a few days. Pick up the bucket and give it a swish every day to help aerate the must and to inhibit mold growth on the surface of the brew.

6. After 3 or 4 days, rack the grapefruit wine from the bucket into the carboy and seal it with the bung and airlock.

7. Label your jug with the brew name and date and set it in a dark place to ferment for a few weeks, or until you no longer see bubbles. Bottle (page 54) when ready.

TIP: Pair your grapefruit wine with toasted raisin bread or a citrus salad with arugula. You can also brighten it up with sugar and soda water for a refreshing spritzer (page 139).

SCARBOROUGH FAIR WINE

This herbal wine is brewed with popular culinary herbs highlighted in a traditional English ballad. "Scarborough Fair" was brought into modern times by Simon & Garfunkel during the folk music revival of the '60s. Being an herbalist, a fan of folk music and an experimental brewer, I couldn't resist giving this one a try!

This wine has a greenish yellow color to it that some may find unpalatable. There are extra raisins in the recipe, since the herbs don't add much in the way of nutrient to the brew. The recipe also calls for less sugar, as this wine is prone to fermenting slowly and leaving a lot of residual sweetness.

1 gal (3.8 L) water, divided

¼ cup (40 g) raisins, chopped

1 lemon, chopped

2 cups (480 ml) strongly brewed black tea

½ cup (20 g) minced fresh parsley

2 heaping tsp (2 g) minced fresh sage (4–6 leaves)

1 heaping tbsp (3 g) fresh minced rosemary (2–3 sprigs)

1 heaping tbsp (3 g) fresh minced thyme

3 cups (600 g) sugar

½ packet (2.5 g) Lalvin D-47 yeast

1.	Gather your ingredients and sanitize your supplies. You'll need a 1- or 2-gallon (3.8- or 7.5-L) stockpot, a long spoon, a straining bag, a funnel, a gallon (3.8-L) carboy, a strainer and a bung and airlock.

2.	Heat ⅔ gallon (2.5 L) of the water in the stockpot with the raisins and lemon until almost boiling. Remove the pot from the heat and add the tea, parsley, sage, rosemary and thyme. Cover the pot with a lid and let the mixture steep for about 15 minutes. Stir in the sugar until it is completely dissolved. Let the must cool until you can safely pour it.

3.	Use the funnel and strainer to transfer the must into the carboy. Top it off with as much of the remaining ⅓ gallon (1.3 L) of water needed for the must to reach the neck of the jug. Seal it with the bung and airlock.

4.	When the glass is cool enough to handle, pitch the yeast. First, cover the mouth of the carboy. Shake the jug for a minute to add oxygen. Sprinkle the yeast into the jug and then recap the carboy with the bung and airlock. Label the jug with the name of the brew and the date and set it aside somewhere out of direct sunlight until it is finished fermenting. Bottle (page 54) when ready.

TIP: Pair this unique herbal brew with goat cheese, cucumbers and a watercress salad on a summer's day!

EARL GREY TEA WINE

I prefer to serve this wine in china teacups alongside lavender pound cake and candied orange peels. The bergamot is front and center in this wine. It is tannic and sweet. The only thing missing is the jot of milk I normally add to my cuppa Earl Grey!

1 gal (3.8 L) water, divided

⅛ cup (20 g) raisins, chopped

½ orange, chopped

8 Earl Grey tea bags

2 lb (910 g) sugar

½ packet (2.5 g) Lalvin K1-V116 yeast

1. Gather your ingredients and sanitize your supplies. You'll need a 1- or 2-gallon (3.8- or 7.5-L) stockpot, a long spoon, a funnel, a strainer, a gallon (3.8-L) carboy and a bung and airlock.

2. Heat ½ gallon (1.9 L) of the water in the stockpot and let it come to a boil. Stir in the raisins, orange and tea bags and remove the pot from the heat. Cover it with a lid and let it steep for 10 minutes.

3. Add the sugar and stir until it is completely dissolved.

4. Use the funnel and strainer to transfer the must into the carboy. Transfer the tea bags from the strainer to the stockpot and stir in the remaining ½ gallon (1.9 L) of water. Add as much of the tea-infused water needed for the must to reach the neck of the jug.

5. When the jug is cool enough to handle, pitch the yeast. First, cover the mouth of the carboy. Shake the jug for a minute to add oxygen. Sprinkle the yeast into the jug and then recap the carboy with the bung and airlock. Label the jug with the name of the brew and the date and set it aside somewhere out of direct sunlight until it is finished fermenting. Bottle (page 54) when ready.

RECIPE NOTE: Make this wine a "Lady Grey" by adding 1 teaspoon of dried lavender flowers and 1 teaspoon orange zest with the tea bags.

TIP: Tie the strings of the tea bags together to make it easier to handle them!

FRUITCAKE WINE

This fruitcake wine is a fortified wine, meaning that it has a strong spirit added to it. Fortification was done in ye olden days to stabilize wine for travel over long distances, and it also serves to cease fermentation. This wine is best served as an after-dinner tipple over the holidays. It pairs well with the scent of turkey and pecan pie, the noise of children having too much fun and the sound of the family arguing over politics.

FOR THE WINE
½ cup (85 g) dried apricots, chopped

1.5 oz (40 g) dried cherries, chopped

½ cup (80 g) raisins, chopped

½ lemon, chopped

1 gal (3.8 L) water, divided

1 stick cinnamon

1 cup (240 ml) strongly brewed black tea

1½ lb (680 g) sugar

½ packet (2.5 g) Lalvin K1-V116 yeast

FOR RACKING
1 vanilla bean, sliced lengthwise

FOR BOTTLING
1 cup (240 ml) brandy

RECIPE NOTE: This wine might not be completely clear due to pectin in the dried fruits. Consider it part of the charm!

1. Gather your ingredients and sanitize your supplies. You'll need a straining bag, a 2-gallon (7.5-L) brew bucket, a 1- or 2-gallon (3.8- or 7.5-L) stockpot, a long spoon, a funnel, a strainer, a gallon (3.8-L) carboy, a racking cane and a bung and airlock.

2. For the wine, put the apricots, cherries, raisins and lemon in the straining bag and set it in the brew bucket.

3. Heat ⅔ gallon (2.5 L) of the water in the stockpot with the cinnamon stick and let it boil for about 5 minutes. Remove the pot from the heat, add the tea and stir in the sugar. Cover the pot with a lid and let the mixture steep for about 10 minutes. Let the must cool until you can safely pour it.

4. Use the funnel and strainer to pour the warm must into the bucket. Add the remaining ⅓ gallon (1.3 L) of water and stir the must. Seal the bucket with the lid and airlock.

5. When the brew bucket is cool enough to handle, pitch the yeast. First, sprinkle the yeast into the brew bucket and stir it in to add oxygen and mix in the yeast. Put the lid onto the bucket, making sure it is sealed, and then put the airlock in place. Label the bucket with the name of the brew and the date and set it aside somewhere out of direct sunlight for 3 to 4 days. Pick up the bucket and give it a gentle swish every day to help keep it mixed and to inhibit mold growth on the surface of the wine.

6. For racking, put the vanilla bean in the carboy. Rack your wine from the bucket into the carboy. Seal it with the bung and airlock and let it work until you no longer see bubbles.

7. For bottling, pour the brandy into a 2-gallon (7.5-L) brew bucket. Taste your wine, and if you want to adjust the sweetness with a syrup (page 143, 144 or 147), add that to the brew bucket as well. Rack the wine over to the bucket, give it a few gentle stirs to ensure that the brandy is evenly mixed in and proceed to bottle (page 54) your fruitcake wine.

RASPBERRY-PEAR WINE

Light pink, sweet and tart, this Raspberry-Pear Wine is a joy to behold. Whether dry or sweet, it makes a lovely picnic wine when paired with chèvre, crackers and fresh fruit.

1 gal (3.8 L) water, divided

⅛ cup (20 g) raisins, chopped

½ lemon, chopped

1 cup (240 ml) strongly brewed black tea

2 lb (910 g) sugar

3 lb (1.4 kg) fresh pears, chopped, frozen and thawed

1 lb (455 g) fresh raspberries, frozen and thawed

½ packet (2.5 g) Lalvin K1-V116 yeast

1.   Gather your ingredients and sanitize your supplies. You'll need a 1- or 2-gallon (3.8- or 7.5-L) stockpot, a long spoon, a straining bag, a 2-gallon (7.5-L) brew bucket, a funnel, a strainer, a gallon (3.8-L) carboy, a racking cane and a bung and airlock.

2.   Heat ⅔ gallon (2.5 L) of the water in the stockpot with the raisins and lemon until almost boiling. Remove the pot from the heat and add the tea. Cover the pot with a lid and let the mixture steep for about 10 minutes. Stir in the sugar until it is completely dissolved.

3.   Put the pears and raspberries in a straining bag and tie it shut. Place it in the bottom of the bucket and gently mash it with your spoon to release the juices. Let the must cool until you can safely pour it. Use the funnel and strainer to pour it into the bucket. Add the remaining ⅓ gallon (1.3 L) of water and stir the must. Seal the bucket with the lid and airlock.

4.   When the brew bucket is cool enough to handle, pitch the yeast. First, sprinkle the yeast into the brew bucket and stir it in to add oxygen and mix in the yeast. Put the lid onto the bucket, making sure it is sealed, and then put the airlock in place. Label the bucket with the name of the brew and the date and set it aside somewhere out of direct sunlight for 3 to 4 days. Pick up the bucket and give it a gentle swish every day to help keep it mixed and to inhibit mold growth on the surface of the wine.

5.   Taste your wine on racking day, since this gives you an opportunity to add a sugar syrup (page 143, 144 or 147) if you want a sweeter brew. Rack your wine from the bucket into the carboy. Seal it with the bung and airlock and let it work until you no longer see bubbles. Bottle (page 54) when ready.

CHOCOLATE-CHERRY WINE

There's something supremely naughty about dark chocolate and rich, tart cherries, and even more so when you add alcohol to the mix! This decadent brew is well worth the work and the wait.

FOR THE WINE
3 lb (1.4 kg) frozen cherries, thawed

1 gal (3.8 L) water, divided

⅛ cup (20 g) raisins, chopped

2 tbsp (18 g) cacao nibs

1½ lb (680 g) sugar

½ packet (2.5 g) Lalvin K1-V116 yeast

FOR RACKING
1 vanilla bean, sliced lengthwise

1. Gather your ingredients and sanitize your supplies. You'll need a straining bag, a 2-gallon (7.5-L) brew bucket, a 1- or 2-gallon (3.8- or 7.5-L) stockpot, a long spoon, a funnel, a strainer, a gallon (3.8-L) carboy, a racking cane and a bung and airlock.

2. For the wine, put the cherries in a straining bag and tie it closed. Set the straining bag in the brew bucket and mash it gently to release some of the fruit juices.

3. Heat ⅔ gallon (2.5 L) of the water in the stockpot with the raisins and let it come to a gentle, rolling boil. Add in the cacao nibs and stir. Boil the must gently for about 5 minutes. Remove the pot from the heat and stir in the sugar until it is completely dissolved. Cover the pot with a lid and let the mixture steep for 10 minutes.

4. Use the funnel and strainer to pour the warm must into the bucket over the cherries. Add the remaining ⅓ gallon (1.3 L) of water and stir the must. Seal the bucket with the lid and airlock.

5. When the brew bucket is cool enough to handle, pitch the yeast. First, sprinkle the yeast into the brew bucket and stir it in to add oxygen and mix in the yeast. Put the lid onto the bucket, making sure it is sealed, and then put the airlock in place. Label the bucket with the name of the brew and the date and set it aside somewhere out of direct sunlight for 3 to 4 days. Pick up the bucket and give it a gentle swish every day to help keep it mixed and to inhibit mold growth on the surface of the wine.

6. For racking day, put the vanilla bean in the carboy. Rack your wine from the bucket into the carboy. Seal it with a bung and airlock and let it work until you no longer see bubbles.

7. Bottle (page 54) when ready, although this particular recipe takes a long time to clear because of the cacao. Be prepared to wait a few months for perfection, if you want your wine to be crystal clear.

Ciders Sweet and Dry

*Oh never, oh never, oh never again. If I live to a hundred or
a hundred-and-ten! I fell to the ground and I couldn't get up after drinking
a pint of the Johnny-Jump-Up!*

—Irish pub song

Cider is a simple name for a complicated creature. It doesn't seem like something as basic as fermented apple juice should have as many variations as it does!

Most people are familiar with the modern version of cider—sparkling and sweet with a strong apple aroma. However, traditional ciders are quite different. They are usually not carbonated and have a higher alcohol potential.

This chapter includes both types of recipes. If you want to brew something sweet, try the Basic Cider (page 83), Perry (page 87) or any recipe that uses ale yeast. Go for the Maple Syrup (page 92) or the Chai-Spiced Cider (page 95) recipes if you want a drier, wine-like cider experience.

Whether you prefer dry or sweet, you should still follow the warning in the Johnny-Jump-Up song—beware the delicious, yet very intoxicating cider! A pint or two can really pack a punch.

AN APPLE A DAY . . .

Apples and pears seem to jump off the tree when they are ripe and ready to be picked. The ground under the trees is littered with fallen fruit, often cracked open and fermenting in the summer sun. Drunken wasps and bees buzz from fruit to fruit, too tipsy to be much of a bother to a forager.

Ciders are best made with healthy, whole fruit, so if you are picking apples or pears, leave the busted ones for the buzzing bugs. When gathering fresh fruit for making cider, use a few different varieties. The more apple flavors that you include—sweet, tart, sour—the richer and better the apple flavor in your cider.

I don't have a fruit mill or cider press, so my cider recipes are made with bottles of juice. If you are lucky, you have orchards in your area and can get unpasteurized, local apple ciders that often come in glass gallon (3.8 L) jugs that are perfect for brewing! If you don't have that nearby, store-bought juice in plastic bottles will do the trick. You must double check the labels on any juice you intend to use for brewing to be sure the juice does not contain preservatives. Citric acid is okay, but other preservatives will keep the yeast from growing.

You can use wine yeasts, such as Lalvin 71B, if you fancy a drier cider. Ale yeasts are popular for brewing lower-alcohol, sweeter modern ciders. The recipes in this chapter include examples of both styles. Try them both, then decide your preference.

MASTER RECIPE: BASIC CIDER

Here's a simple recipe to help you get started on the boozy apple path. It honestly doesn't get much easier than this! You can produce a drinkable cider from this base recipe. When you've got it mastered, you can get creative!

This recipe is made from a gallon (3.8-L) of unfiltered apple juice in a plastic jug. You can use white sugar, but I prefer brown sugar, which imparts a bit of dark caramel flavor and color to the final product.

1 gal (3.8 L) apple juice, divided

1½ cups (330 g) packed brown sugar

1 tsp (2.5 g) Safale S-04 dry ale yeast

1 oz (28 g) priming sugar, optional

1. **Gather and sanitize equipment:** Gather your ingredients and sanitize your supplies. For this recipe, you'll need a 2-cup (480-ml) liquid measuring cup, a funnel, a gallon (3.8-L) carboy and a bung and airlock.

2. **Make the brew:** Open the apple juice, pour 2 cups (480 ml) into the measuring cup and set it aside. Add the brown sugar to the apple juice container. Close the container and shake it until all of the sugar is completely dissolved.

3. **Add the yeast:** Open the container and pitch the yeast directly into the apple juice. Close the container and shake it again to aerate the must and wake up the yeast.

4. **Funnel:** Using the funnel, pour the must from the plastic container into the carboy. If needed, top off the carboy with as much of the remaining 2 cups (480 ml) of apple juice needed for the must to reach the neck of the jug. Seal it off with a bung and airlock. Label the jug with the brew name and date.

5. **Ferment:** Let the brew ferment until the cider has cleared.

6. **Bottle:** After the cider has cleared and fermentation has stopped, it is time to bottle your cider. You have a few options at this point depending on if you want a still cider or a carbonated cider.

7. **If you want a still cider,** go ahead and bottle it (page 84) as it is.

(continued)

8. **If you prefer your cider to be sparkling,** use priming sugar during bottling to give you bubbles. Sanitize a 2-gallon (7.5-L) brew bucket, a long spoon and a racking cane or siphon tube. Bring ½ cup (120 ml) of water to a boil in a small pan. Stir in the priming sugar until it is completely dissolved, reduce the heat and simmer the syrup for 5 minutes. Pour the syrup into the bottom of the brew bucket. Siphon the cider from the jug into the brew bucket; avoid transferring the trub sediment from the bottom. Stir the cider gently to ensure the syrup is mixed in evenly before bottling.

9. **Bottle:** To bottle your cider, first sanitize your racking cane, caps and bottles. Use the racking cane or siphon tube to fill the bottles just up to the neck. Cap your bottles and label them.

10. **Age:** Store your bottles of cider upright in a dark, warm area for at least 2 weeks. If you added priming sugar, the cider will carbonate in the bottles.

11. **Mellow:** Sharp, vinegary flavors are common in young ciders and will often mellow out with age. Don't worry! The longer you age your cider, the better it will taste. Try a bottle after a few weeks and see how it is coming along.

TIP: Because this cider is brewed with ale yeast, there should definitely be some residual sweetness. The procedure in step 8 will not add sweetness—there is only enough sugar to carbonate the cider in the bottles.

PERRY (PEAR CIDER)

Apples make cider and pears make perry. This version is made easy by using bottled fruit juice from the market, but I dream of finding a fresh gallon (3.8-L) jug of real, unfiltered pear juice to use. Store-bought pear juice tends to be thick and pulpy, leaving you with an opaque brew.

1 gal (3.8 L) pear juice, divided

1 cup (200 g) packed brown sugar

1 cup (240 ml) strongly brewed black tea

1 tsp (2.5 g) Safale S-04 dry ale yeast

1. Gather your ingredients and sanitize your supplies. For this recipe, you'll need a 1- or 2-gallon (3.8- or 7.5-L) stockpot, a long spoon, a funnel, a strainer, a gallon (3.8-L) carboy and a bung and airlock.

2. Warm ½ gallon (1.9 L) of the pear juice in the stockpot, but don't let it boil or you run the risk of creating a pectin haze. Add the brown sugar and tea, and stir until the sugar is completely dissolved.

3. Using a funnel and strainer, pour the warmed pear juice into the carboy and top it off with as much of the remaining ½ gallon (1.9 L) of bottled juice needed for the must to reach the neck of the jug. Pitch the yeast and give the must a few good shakes to aerate it and wake up the yeast.

4. Seal the carboy with the bung and airlock. Label the jug with the brew name and date. Bottle (page 84) when fermentation is done. You will know the cider's ready for bottling when it no longer bubbles, as you can't check for completion by opacity for this cider.

ORANGE-HIBISCUS CIDER

This bright, tart cider uses a syrup infused with fruit and herbs to add complexity and a bit of extra sweetness to the table. If you want to feel fancy, garnish your glasses with a slice of orange and hibiscus flowers.

I enjoy this best poolside on a summer's day while relaxing in the sunshine.

1 cup (240 ml) water

1 orange, zested and juiced, divided

2 tbsp (5 g) dried hibiscus petals

1 cup (200 g) packed brown sugar

1 gal (3.8 L) apple juice

1 tsp (2.5 g) Safale S-04 dry ale yeast

1. Gather your ingredients and sanitize your supplies. For this recipe, you'll need a small saucepan, a long spoon, a strainer, a gallon (3.8-L) carboy, a funnel and a bung and airlock.

2. In the saucepan, bring the water to a boil, and add the orange zest and hibiscus petals. Let that simmer for about 5 minutes. Remove the pan from the heat and add the brown sugar, stirring until it is completely dissolved. Strain the syrup into the carboy. Add the orange juice to the carboy.

3. Using the funnel, add the apple juice to the carboy until the must reaches the neck of the jug. Put your hand over the mouth of the jug and give it a few good shakes to mix everything.

4. Pitch the yeast in the carboy. Seal it off with a bung and airlock. Shake it again to aerate the must and wake up the yeast.

5. Label the jug with the brew name and date. After the cider has cleared and fermentation has stopped, you can bottle (page 84) your cider to be still or sparkling.

DARK GINGER CIDER

Molasses, ginger and apples are a natural grouping for autumn and winter flavors.
Dark, spicy and rich, this cider pairs beautifully with sweet potatoes or pumpkin pie.
You should also try it warmed in a mug with a bit of honey and fortified with a splash of dark rum.

2 cups (480 ml) water

3½ oz (100 g) fresh ginger, thinly sliced

¼ cup (80 g) molasses

1 cup (200 g) packed brown sugar

1 gal (3.8 L) apple juice

1 tsp (2.5 g) Safale S-04 dry ale yeast

1. Gather your ingredients and sanitize your supplies. For this recipe, you'll need a saucepan, a long spoon, a strainer, a gallon (3.8-L) carboy, a funnel and a bung and airlock.

2. In the saucepan, mix the water, ginger, molasses and brown sugar, then bring the mixture to a boil over medium heat. Stir to combine the ingredients well. Reduce the heat to low and let the mixture simmer, until it is reduced by half into a dark, spicy syrup. Strain the syrup into the carboy.

3. Using the funnel, pour the apple juice into the carboy on top of the syrup. Cover the mouth of the jug and shake it well to get everything mixed together.

4. Pitch the yeast into the jug and shake it again to aerate the must and wake up the yeast. Seal the jug with the bung and airlock. Label the carboy with the brew name and date.

5. After the cider has cleared and fermentation has stopped, you can bottle (page 84) your cider. If it is slow to clear, you can rack the cider to a clean carboy. Check it weekly to see how it is getting along. The choice of bottling this still or sparkling is up to you!

MAPLE SYRUP CIDER

Maple syrup and apples are just perfect together. The tart, sharp apples and the silky, sweet maple blend in this brew to make a very classy dry cider. Pair this cider with crumbly white cheddar, maple-bacon flavored treats or smoked nuts.

1 gal (3.8 L) apple juice, divided

2 cups (480 ml) maple syrup

½ cup (100 g) packed brown sugar

1 cup (240 ml) strongly brewed black tea

½ packet (2.5 g) Lalvin 71B yeast

1. Gather your ingredients and sanitize your supplies. For this recipe, you'll need a 1- or 2-gallon (3.8- or 7.5-L) stockpot, a long spoon, a funnel, a strainer, a gallon (3.8-L) carboy, a raking cane and a bung and airlock.

2. Warm ½ gallon (1.9 L) of the apple juice in the stockpot, but only to about 90°F (32°C). Don't let it boil or you run the risk of creating a pectin haze from the apple juice. Add the maple syrup, brown sugar and tea and stir until it is all mixed well.

3. Using the funnel and strainer, pour the warmed apple juice mixture into the carboy and top it off with as much of the remaining ½ gallon (1.9 L) of apple juice needed for the must to reach the neck of the jug. Pitch the yeast, cover the mouth of the jug and give it a few good shakes to aerate the must and wake up the yeast.

4. Seal it with the bung and airlock. Label the jug with the brew name and date. After 2 weeks, rack it over to a new sanitized carboy to get it off of the lees and help it start to clear.

5. Bottle (page 84) your cider after it has cleared and fermentation has stopped. Since this cider is brewed with wine yeast and has a higher potential alcohol, you shouldn't try to carbonate it unless you plan on bottling in champagne bottles with wire clamps! Save the priming sugar for the ciders made with ale yeast.

RECIPE NOTE: This still cider is neither mellow nor maple-flavored at bottling, but it changes quickly! At two weeks, the dry cider will mellow out and reveal the maple aroma and flavor that you hoped for. Wonderful when dry, Maple Syrup Cider is just as delicious with a bit of Basic Simple Syrup (page 143) or maple syrup added to the glass at serving.

CHAI-SPICED CIDER

Forget the chai latte or hot mug of tea—this Chai-Spiced Cider is delicious dry or sweet, warm or cold. The warmth from the ginger and black pepper lift the cinnamon and cardamom to make an invigorating glass of cider!

1 cup (240 ml) water

⅛ cup (20 g) raisins, chopped

1 cup (60 g) chopped fresh ginger

2 sticks cinnamon

¼ tsp cardamom

⅛ tsp black pepper

2 black tea bags

1 cup (240 ml) boiling water

1 cup (200 g) packed brown sugar

1 gal (3.8 L) apple juice

½ packet (2.5 g) Lalvin 71B yeast

1. Gather your ingredients and sanitize your supplies. For this recipe, you'll need a small pot, a long spoon, a funnel, a strainer, a gallon (3.8-L) carboy and a bung and airlock.

2. Put the water, raisins, ginger, cinnamon, cardamom and black pepper in the small pot and bring the mixture to a boil. Steep the tea bags in 1 cup (240 ml) of boiling water for 5 minutes and add the tea to the pot. Remove the pot from the heat, add the brown sugar and stir until it is completely dissolved.

3. Use the funnel and strainer to pour the spiced syrup into the carboy. Add as much of the apple juice needed for the must to reach the neck of the carboy. Cover the mouth of the jug and give it a few good shakes to mix it up.

4. Open the jug and pitch the yeast directly into the must. Close the jug and shake it again to aerate the must and wake up the yeast.

5. Seal the jug with the bung and airlock. Label the jug with the brew name and date. After 2 weeks, rack it over to a new sanitized carboy to get it off the lees and help it start to clear.

6. Bottle (page 84) your cider after it has cleared and fermentation has stopped.

SUMMER BERRY CIDER

There are wild berry brambles in the hedgerows around my yard. I harvest tart blackberries and sweet black raspberries by the handful every day and stash them away in freezer bags. Once the season shifts toward the colder months, I can see what I've managed to save and decide how to use them!

This tart, dry cider is racked onto a pound (455 g) of foraged summer fruits—try blackberries, black raspberries, wineberries, blueberries or mulberries—to make something truly beautiful.

FOR THE CIDER

1 gal (3.8 L) apple juice, divided

1 cup (240 ml) strongly brewed black tea

½ cup (100 g) packed brown sugar

1 tsp (2.5 g) Safale S-04 dry ale yeast

FOR RACKING

1 lb (455 g) mixed berries, frozen and thawed

RECIPE NOTE: Summer Berry Cider is delightful when bottled as is, but it excels when it is bottled with priming sugar (page 84) so that it has some sparkle!

1. Gather your ingredients and sanitize your supplies. For this recipe, you'll need a 1- or 2-gallon (3.8- or 7.5-L) stockpot, a long spoon, a funnel, a strainer, a gallon (3.8-L) carboy, a straining bag, a 2-gallon (7.5-L) brew bucket, a racking cane and a bung and airlock.

2. For the cider, warm ½ gallon (1.9 L) of the apple juice in the stockpot, but only to about 90°F (32°C). Don't let the juice boil or you run the risk of creating a pectin haze from the apple juice. Add the tea and brown sugar, and stir until it is all mixed well.

3. Using the funnel and strainer, pour the warmed apple juice mixture into the carboy and top it off with as much of the remaining ½ gallon (1.9 L) of the apple juice for the must to reach the neck of the jug. Pitch the yeast, cover the mouth of the jug and give it a few good shakes to aerate the must and wake up the yeast.

4. Seal the jug with the bung and airlock. Label the jug with the brew name and date and let the wine ferment for 2 weeks.

5. For racking, put the fruit in the straining bag. Place the bag in the brew bucket and press it with the spoon to release the juices. Rack the cider from the carboy into the brew bucket, avoiding the lees at the bottom of the jug.

6. Give the berries a few days to infuse into the cider before bottling. Pick up the bucket and give it a swish daily to make sure that there is no mold growth on the surface of the cider. Bottle (page 84) when ready.

DRY-HOPPED CIDER

Cider is a bit too sweet for some people, or they find the flavor profile unsophisticated for their refined tastes. You can convert these types with a dry-hopped cider—just a bit of well-balanced bitterness adds complexity and balance to the tart apple notes.

Play around with the hops and yeast options to make this recipe your own. You'll get great results if you stick to varieties of hops with strong notes of citrus and fruity aromas, such as Cascade, Simcoe, Lemondrop or Mosaic. I chose a Belgian yeast for this recipe because the bold character supports the hoppy bitterness by boosting the fruit esters.

FOR THE CIDER
1 gal (3.8 L) apple juice, divided

1 cup (200 g) packed brown sugar

1 tsp (2.5 g) Belgian yeast

FOR RACKING
3 g Cascade hops pellets

1. Gather your ingredients and sanitize your supplies. For this recipe, you'll need a 2-cup (480-ml) liquid measuring cup, a funnel, a gallon (3.8-L) carboy, a racking cane and a bung and airlock.

2. For the cider, pour 2 cups (480 ml) of the apple juice into the measuring cup and set it aside.

3. Add the sugar to the apple juice container. Close the container and shake it until all of the brown sugar has completely dissolved.

4. Open the container and pitch the yeast directly into the apple juice container. Close it and shake it again to aerate the must and wake up the yeast.

5. Using the funnel, pour the must from the container into the carboy. If needed, add the reserved 2 cups (480 ml) apple juice so the must reaches the neck of the jug.

6. Seal it off with the bung and airlock. Label the jug with the brew name and date and let it ferment for 2 weeks.

7. Rack the cider into the carboy and add the hops pellets. Seal the jug with the bung and airlock.

8. Leave the hops in the brew for anywhere from 3 to 7 days, occasionally pulling a taste with a sanitized wine thief to see how the cider is progressing. Remember that every time you open the jug to taste it, you chance contamination, so do so sparingly. When you taste as much citrus and fruit from the hops as you like, bottle (page 84) the brew. Dry-Hopped Cider gets more rave reviews when it is carbonated in the bottle, rather than bottled still.

TIP: Save yourself a mess by using a sanitized straining bag for the hops pellets.

FLOWER GARDEN CIDER

There's something magical about drinking flower petals. It makes me want to put on a crown made of ivy and go frolic in the fields with the butterflies!

This cider is made with dried flowers: calendula for the earthy notes and bright color, chamomile to complement the apple notes and provide a bit of bitterness, yarrow to give a sharp bite and tannins and rose petals to lend their floral tones to the whole profile.

1 cup (240 ml) water

⅓ cup (3 g) dried calendula flowers

1½ tbsp (2 g) dried chamomile flowers

1 tbsp (1 g) dried yarrow flowers

1 tbsp (1 g) dried rose petals

1 cup (200 g) sugar

1 gal (3.8 L) apple juice

1 tsp (2.5 g) Safale S-04 dry ale yeast

1 oz (28 g) priming sugar

1. Gather your ingredients and sanitize your supplies. For this recipe, you'll need a small saucepan, a long spoon, a funnel, a strainer, a gallon (3.8-L) carboy, a racking cane and a bung and airlock.

2. Boil the water in a small saucepan and add the calendula, chamomile, yarrow and rose. Remove the pan from the heat, cover it and let it steep for 5 minutes. Add the sugar and stir until it is completely dissolved.

3. Using a funnel and strainer, strain the syrup into the carboy and pour in enough apple juice for the must to reach the neck of the jug. Cover the mouth of the jug and give it a few good shakes to mix everything.

4. Pitch the yeast in the carboy. Seal it with the bung and airlock. Shake the jug again to aerate the must and wake up the yeast.

5. Label the jug with the brew name and date. After 2 weeks, rack the cider into a new sanitized carboy to help it clear. Let the cider finish fermentation and bottle (page 84) when ready. This cider is best with a bit of bubble, so carbonate with the priming sugar (page 84).

ROSE CIDER

Not rosé, but rose! This floral dream of a cider is meant to be strong and dry. A little bit of sweetness is nice, but it can be added as a sugar syrup (page 143, 144 or 147) at the time of serving to suit the palate of the drinker. The aroma from the rose petals and vanilla bean are heady and lush, making this a fantastic cider for a romantic occasion, like a sunset picnic in the park.

FOR THE CIDER
1 cup (240 ml) water
½ cup (6 g) rose petals
1 cup (200 g) sugar
1 gal (3.8 L) apple juice
½ packet (2.5 g) Lalvin 71B yeast

FOR RACKING
1 vanilla bean, sliced lengthwise

1. Gather your ingredients and sanitize your supplies. For this recipe, you'll need a small saucepan, a long spoon, a strainer, a funnel, a gallon (3.8-L) carboy, a racking cane and a bung and airlock.

2. For the cider, boil the water in a small saucepan and add the rose petals. Remove from the heat, cover the pan with a lid and let the mixture steep for 5 minutes. Add the sugar and stir until it is completely dissolved. Strain the syrup into the carboy.

3. Using a funnel, pour enough apple juice into the carboy for the must to reach the neck of the jug. Put your hand over the mouth of the jug and give it a few good shakes to mix everything.

4. Pitch the yeast in the carboy. Seal it off with the bung and airlock. Shake it again to aerate the must and wake up the yeast.

5. Label the jug with the brew name and date and let it ferment for 2 weeks.

6. Rack the cider into the carboy. Add the vanilla bean. Let the cider finish fermentation and bottle (page 84) it still for best results.

MALTED CIDER

Now we will cross the line between two types of brews: ciders and beers. Instead of white or brown sugar, this recipe uses dried malt extract to sweeten the brew. Dried malt extract is more commonly used to provide fermentable sugars in beer recipes.

If you are fond of beers and find ciders to be too light or thin in body, using grains or malts in your cider just might fit the bill.

2 cups (480 ml) water

4 oz (115 g) light dried malt extract

1 gal (3.8 L) apple juice

1 tsp (2.5 g) Safale S-04 dry ale yeast

1.　Gather your ingredients and sanitize your supplies. For this recipe, you'll need a saucepan, a long spoon, a funnel, a gallon (3.8-L) carboy, a racking cane and a bung and airlock.

2.　Boil the water in the saucepan and add the dried malt extract. Stir until it is completely dissolved and then use the funnel to pour the mixture into the carboy. Pour enough apple juice into the carboy for the liquid to reach the neck. Cover and give the jug a few good shakes to make sure the must is well mixed.

3.　Pitch the yeast in the carboy. Seal it with the bung and airlock. Shake the jug again to aerate the must and wake up the yeast.

4.　Label the jug with the brew name and date. After 2 weeks, rack the cider into a new sanitized carboy to help it clear. Let the cider finish fermentation and bottle (page 84) when ready. Malted Cider tastes best with a bit of bubble, so carbonate it with priming sugar (page 84). You might even get a foamy head when you pour it, as with a beer!

Grains and Gruits and Hops, Oh My!

The huntsman, he can't hunt the fox
Nor so loudly to blow his horn
And the tinker he can't mend kettle nor pot
Without a little Barleycorn.
–"John Barleycorn," British folk song

The brewing of beer is a bit more complicated than that of wine, mead and cider. There are malts, grains and bittering agents to consider. The brewing of beer has more steps than the other recipes we've covered so far, but don't worry. You don't need a spreadsheet or lab equipment to brew a good beer, but there's something to be said for the scientific method and good record keeping!

The recipes in this chapter are easy and are based on very basic beer varieties that are well-known, but with an herbal kick, like Thyme and Honey Saison (page 117), Root Beer Brown Ale (page 118), Lemon-Pepper IPA (page 121) and a Cherry Red Ale (page 114).

Once you've played with enough beer recipes to have an idea of the techniques you prefer and the styles of beer you enjoy, you can expand into the territory of crafting your own recipes.

TO HOP, OR NOT TO HOP?

Water, barley, yeast and hops. That simple combination of ingredients comprises our modern understanding of the immensely popular beverage called beer, from the ubiquitous big brand, light beers, to the weirdest and wildest craft brews.

However, we must consider how long humanity has been brewing beer and rethink that tiny list of ingredients. Before the *Reinheitsgebot*, the Bavarian Purity Laws outlined in 1516 that defined and mandated the ingredients that were allowed in beer, it was a very different craft.

Other herbs were used as bittering agents before hops became so commonly used. Herbs like mugwort, yarrow, sweet gale, bog rosemary and wormwood were added to brews to lend their flavors, aroma and herbal properties to the mixture. Many of these herbs have psychoactive, analgesic or stimulating properties that they impart to the beer. These un-hopped beers are called "gruits."

If you need beer-brewing ingredients and supplies and you don't have a local homebrew store to visit, check online! I have used Great Fermentations and also purchased supplies from homebrew stores who list their wares on Amazon. You can find small quantities of hops, grains, herbs and other adjuncts that will work well for 1-gallon (3.8-L) brews.

Oh! An important note: While spent grains are edible for humans and other animals (page 148), please beware of how you dispose of your hop sludge after brew day, as hops are very toxic to dogs. It is hard not to indulge a dog begging for a sip, but sharing a beer with your dog can make them very sick.

MASTER RECIPE: AMERICAN PILSNER

For years, I thought that "beer" meant only the pale, yellow pilsner that was enjoyed by the adults around me. I remember stealing sips as a kid and deciding that it was awful and that I would never like beer.

So, it is with a wry laugh that I present a classic American pilsner for our first foray into beer-brewing together. It is low in alcohol, pale in color and has almost no bitterness. This is a light, refreshing lunch beer, the perfect beer for mowing the lawn and the easiest of all of my beer recipes to share with you.

FOR THE BEER

1½ gal (5.7 L) water

4 oz (115 g) Pale 2-row (specialty grain)

12 oz (340 g) Pilsen light dried malt extract

4 oz (115 g) rice syrup solids (fermentable sugar)

2 g Cascade hops pellets

1 tsp (2.5 g) Safale S-04 dry ale yeast

FOR BOTTLING

½ cup (120 ml) water

1 oz (28 g) priming sugar

1. **Gather and sanitize equipment:** Gather your ingredients and sanitize your equipment. You'll need a 2-gallon (7.5-L) stockpot, a thermometer, a grain bag, a long spoon, a strainer, a bowl, a 2-gallon (7.5-L) brew bucket, a racking cane or siphon tube, a gallon (3.8-L) carboy and a bung and airlock.

2. **For the beer, steep the grains:** Heat the water in the stockpot until it reaches 150 to 160°F (65 to 71°C). If the water gets hotter, you run the risk of leaching bitter flavors from the grain. Pour the Pale 2-row grains into the grain bag, tie a loose knot at the top and put them into the pot to steep. Stir the water regularly to ensure that the grain bag is not getting stuck at the bottom of the hot pot. After 30 minutes, remove the grain bag, and let it drain back into the pot while you prepare for the next steps. For draining, I tie the grain bag to the pot handle or the long spoon, set over the pot. When you remove the grains from the bag, you can put them in the strainer set over the bowl to dry for use in other recipes (page 148). The liquid left in the stockpot is your wort.

3. **Boil the wort:** Bring your wort to a gentle, rolling boil. Add the dried malt extract and the rice syrup solids and stir until the wort returns to a gentle boil. Next, you'll add the hops. You'll sometimes have to add ingredients, such as multiple hops and spices, at different times. With this master recipe, there's only one round. Add the hops and let them boil for an hour. Near the end of the hour, fill a sink with ice water. Remove the pot from the heat and place it in the ice water in the sink. Let the wort cool until it is near 70°F (21°C).

(continued)

4.   **Ferment:** Use the racking cane or siphon tube to transfer the wort into the brew bucket. Be careful to avoid transferring the hop sludge from the bottom of the brew pot. Sprinkle the yeast into the wort and stir it. Put on the bucket lid, add the airlock, label your brew and store it in an area around 64 to 72°F (18 to 22°C) out of direct sunlight for 2 to 3 days.

It is easiest to ferment in a brew bucket for the first few days, but if you don't have a bucket, primary fermentation can take place in a 1-gallon (3.8-L) jug. Be warned that beer fermentation is very active compared to wines, meads and ciders, so if you ferment in the jug, you should use a blow-off tube instead of an airlock for the first couple of days. Make a blow-off tube by inserting one end of a 3-foot (91-cm) long piece of ¼-inch (6-mm) rubber tubing into the bung in the jug, and the other end of the tubing into a bowl of sanitized water placed next to the jug. Once the fermentation has calmed a few days later, replace the tube with a standard airlock and let your beer finish fermenting as usual.

5.   **Rack:** About a week after brew day, carefully transfer the beer from the bucket into the jug, avoiding the lees at the bottom. Return the carboy to the same dark, warm place and wait for another 2 weeks for fermentation to finish.

6.   **Bottle and carbonate:** Sanitize your caps and bottles. To get bubbles in your glass, you must prime the beer with a fermentable sugar at the time of bottling. Bring ½ cup (120 ml) of water to a boil in a small pan. Stir in the priming sugar until it is completely dissolved, reduce the heat and simmer the syrup for 5 minutes. Pour that sugar syrup into the bottom of the brew bucket. Siphon the beer from the jug into the bucket, avoiding the sediment from the bottom of the jug. Stir the beer gently to ensure the sugar is mixed in evenly. Use the racking cane to fill the beer bottles. Cap your bottles and label them.

7.   **Age:** Store your bottles of beer upright for 2 weeks. The beer will carbonate in the bottles. Try one, and if the carbonation seems flat or the flavor is a bit off, don't worry. Just let the bottles sit and age for another week and then try another bottle. It's amazing what a bit of time can do to change a brew.

GRUIT ALE

Before hops were mandated for beer production by the Reinheitsgebot, there were centuries worth of alternative bittering agents used in brewing. Roots, spices and herbs not only flavored beers, they imparted their medicinal properties. In this recipe, I've blended bitter and herbaceous yarrow with the sharp and piney juniper berries, offsetting them with the aromatic aniseed to make an interesting and palatable gruit ale.

Try pairing this with a sourdough bread with salted butter, roasted neeps (turnip) and taters and a lamb chop to be transported back in time.

1½ gal (5.7 L) water

6 oz (170 g) caramel 60L malt

1 lb (455 g) golden light dried malt extract

½ cup (5 g) yarrow flowers

½ tsp (1 g) aniseed

⅔ tbsp (3 g) juniper berries

2 tbsp (40 g) honey

½ packet (2.5 g) dry ale yeast

TIP: Traditionally, gruit ale was not carbonated, as modern beer is. Bottle some of this brew flat and bottle others with priming sugar (page 110) to see which you prefer.

1. Gather your ingredients and sanitize your equipment. You'll need a 2-gallon (3.8-L) stockpot, a thermometer, a grain bag, a long spoon, a racking cane or siphon tube, a 2-gallon (7.5-L) brew bucket, a gallon (3.8-L) carboy and a bung and airlock.

2. Heat the water in the stockpot until it reaches 150 to 160°F (65 to 71°C). Pour the caramel malt grains into a grain bag, tie a loose knot at the top and steep them in the pot for 20 minutes while keeping the water temperature between 150 and 160°F (65 to 71°C). Remove the grain bag and let it drain back into the pot while you prepare for the next steps.

3. Bring your wort to a gentle, rolling boil. Add the dried malt extract and stir until the wort returns to a gentle boil. Add the yarrow and aniseed and boil for 30 minutes. Add the juniper berries and simmer for another 30 minutes. Near the end of this 30 minutes, fill a sink with ice water. Stir the honey into the wort. Cover the pot, remove it from the heat and place the whole pot in the ice water in the sink. Let the wort cool until it is near 70°F (21°C).

4. Use the racking cane to siphon the wort into the bucket, avoiding transferring the herbal sludge from the brew pot. Sprinkle the yeast into the wort and stir it. Put on the bucket lid, add the airlock, label your brew and store it in an area around 64 to 72°F (18 to 22°C) out of direct sunlight for 4 to 6 days.

5. Carefully transfer the beer into the jug, again avoiding the lees at the bottom of the bucket. Return the jug to the dark, warm place and wait for 2 weeks. Bottle (page 110) when ready.

CHERRY RED ALE

This is a brightly colored and flavored beer made with fresh fruit. The cherry flavor is present without being overwhelming or too sweet, balanced by the bitterness of the hops and a hint of spice. This is a fruity beer that can still be enjoyed by those who normally consider them too "froofy," or fancy.

1½ gal (5.7 L) water

6 oz (170 g) caramel 80L malt

20 oz (570 g) Pilsen light dried malt extract

3 crushed allspice berries

12 cracked grain of paradise seeds

3 g El Dorado hops pellets

2 g Cascade hops pellets

1 lb (455 g) fresh cherries, pitted

1 tsp (2.5 g) Safale S-04 dry ale yeast

TIP: If you can't find grain of paradise, substitute with one-quarter part of black peppercorns. For example, 12 grain of paradise seeds equal 3 black peppercorns.

1. Gather your ingredients and sanitize your equipment. You'll need a 2-gallon (7.5-L) stockpot, a thermometer, a grain bag, a long spoon, a straining bag, a 2-gallon (7.5-L) brew bucket, a racking cane or siphon tube, a gallon (3.8-L) carboy and a bung and airlock.

2. Heat the water in the stockpot until it reaches 150 to 160°F (65 to 71°C). Pour the caramel malt grains into the grain bag, tie a loose knot at the top, and steep them in the pot for 20 minutes, while keeping the temperature between 150 and 160°F (65 to 71°C). Remove the grain bag and let it drain back into the pot while you prepare for the next steps.

3. Bring your wort to a gentle, rolling boil. Add the dried malt extract and stir until the wort returns to a gentle boil. Add the allspice, grain of paradise seeds and El Dorado hops and let those boil for 30 minutes. Add the Cascade hops and boil for another 30 minutes. Near the end of the 30 minutes, fill a sink with ice water. Remove the pot from the heat and place it in the ice water in the sink. Let the wort cool until it is near 70°F (21°C).

4. Pour the cherries into the straining bag and tie it shut. Place it on the bottom of the fermenting bucket and use a potato masher, or similar implement, to carefully crush the cherries and release some of the juices. Use the racking cane to siphon the wort into the bucket, avoiding the hop sludge on the bottom of the brew pot. Sprinkle the yeast into the wort and stir it. Put on the bucket lid, add the airlock, label your brew and store it in an area around 64 to 72°F (18 to 22°C) out of direct sunlight for 2 to 3 days.

5. Once the fermentation slows, carefully transfer the beer into the jug, again avoiding the lees at the bottom of the bucket. Let it work for 2 weeks. Bottle (page 110) when ready.

THYME AND HONEY SAISON

If you enjoy beers that are rich, golden and complex, this is the saison for you!
The taste of this traditional, thick farmhouse ale is lifted with a bit of honey and
freshly minced thyme added at the end of the boil.

It is difficult to taste the herbal notes of this brew if you sample it at bottling, but don't worry—after two or
three weeks in the bottle, the thyme comes shining through!

1½ gal (5.7 L) water

4 oz (115 g) caramel 80L malt

1 lb (455 g) light dried malt extract

6 g El Dorado hops pellets, divided

2 oz (55 g) Candi sugar

2 tbsp (5 g) fresh thyme leaves, minced

2 tbsp (40 g) honey

½ packet (2.5 g) Belgian saison yeast

1. Gather your ingredients and sanitize your equipment. You'll need a 2-gallon (7.5-L) stockpot, a thermometer, a grain bag, a long spoon, a racking cane or siphon tube, a 2-gallon (7.5-L) brew bucket, a gallon (3.8-L) carboy and a bung and airlock.

2. Heat the water in the stockpot until it reaches 150 to 160°F (65 to 71°C). Pour the caramel malt grains into the grain bag, tie a loose knot at the top and steep them in the pot for 20 minutes, while keeping the temperature between 150 and 160°F (65 to 71°C). Remove the grain bag and let it drain back into the pot while you prepare for the next steps.

3. Bring your wort to a gentle, rolling boil. Add the dried malt extract and stir until the wort returns to a gentle boil. Add half of the hops and let those boil for 45 minutes. Add the Candi sugar and boil for 5 minutes. Add the remaining hops and boil another 5 minutes. Finally, stir in the thyme and honey. Near the end of the last 5 minutes of boiling, fill a sink with ice water. Cover the pot, remove it from the heat and place the whole pot in the ice water in the sink. Let the wort cool until it is near 70°F (21°C).

4. Use the racking cane to siphon the wort into the bucket, avoiding the trub on the bottom of the brew pot. Sprinkle the yeast into the wort and stir it. Put on the bucket lid, add the airlock, label your brew and store it in an area around 64 to 72°F (18 to 22°C) out of direct sunlight for 4 to 6 days.

5. Carefully transfer the beer into the jug, again avoiding the lees at the bottom of the bucket. Return the jug to the dark, warm place and wait for 2 weeks. Bottle (page 110) when ready.

ROOT BEER BROWN ALE

Root beer is near and dear to my heart. This North American soft drink is traditionally flavored with sassafras or sarsaparilla, and other roots and barks known for their tonic qualities. While sassafras is considered dangerous in vast quantities and is not legally permitted for commercially produced products in the United States, sassafras herb is legal to purchase and use on your own.

The brown ale base takes on the flavors and aroma of root beer without the prevailing sweetness. Feel free to add wintergreen, spruce, vanilla, anise, nutmeg or fenugreek— the list of useful tonic roots and herbs used in root beer is long.

1½ gal (5.7 L) water

3 oz (85 g) caramel 120L malt

3 oz (85 g) brown malt

20 oz (570 g) light dried malt extract

6 g El Dorado hops pellets, divided

3 g Nugget hops pellets

¼ cup (20 g) sarsaparilla

1 tbsp (3 g) sassafras

3 tsp (3 g) birch bark

2 tsp (2 g) chicory root

1 whole star anise

1 tsp (2.5 g) Safale S-04 dry ale yeast

1. Gather your ingredients and sanitize your equipment. You'll need a 2-gallon (7.5-L) stockpot, a thermometer, a grain bag, a long spoon, a racking cane or siphon tube, a 2-gallon (7.5-L) brew bucket, a gallon (3.8-L) carboy and a bung and airlock.

2. Heat the water in the stockpot until it reaches 150 to 160°F (65 to 71°C). Pour the caramel and brown malt into the grain bag, tie a loose knot at the top and steep them in the pot for about 20 minutes, while keeping the water temperature between 150 and 160°F (65 to 71°C). Remove the grain bag and let it drain back into the pot while you prepare for the next steps.

3. Bring your wort to a gentle, rolling boil. Add the dried malt extract and stir until the wort returns to a gentle boil. Add half of the El Dorado hops and let those boil for 40 minutes. Add the Nugget hops and boil for 10 minutes. Add the remaining El Dorado hops, the sarsaparilla, sassafras, birch bark, chicory root and star anise. Simmer for a final 5 minutes. While the wort is simmering, fill a sink with ice water. Remove the pot from the heat and place it in the ice water in the sink. Let the wort cool until it is near 70°F (21°C).

4. Use the racking cane to siphon your wort into the bucket. Sprinkle the yeast into the wort and stir it. Put on the bucket lid, add the airlock, label your brew and store it in an area around 64 to 72°F (18 to 22°C) out of direct sunlight for 3 to 4 days.

5. Carefully transfer the beer into the carboy, avoiding the lees at the bottom of the bucket. Let it work for another 2 weeks. Bottle (page 110) when ready.

LEMON-PEPPER IPA

I'm from the southeastern corner of Virginia, where the Atlantic Ocean meets the Chesapeake Bay, so I grew up eating fresh fish and blue crabs by the bushel! This hoppy, strong beer is perfect for those hot summer days of shelling crabs and laughing with friends.

Lemon zest lends a bright note to the strong bitters in this solid IPA, while the black pepper gives a spicy flavor that grows stronger with each sip.

1½ gal (5.7 L) water

3 oz (85 g) caramel 30L malt

3 oz (85 g) biscuit malt

20 oz (570 g) Pilsen light dried malt extract

5 g Nugget hops pellets

6 g Chinook hops pellets, divided

1 lemon, zested and juiced

1 tsp black pepper

1 tsp (2.5 g) Safale S-04 dry ale yeast

1. Gather your ingredients and sanitize your equipment. You'll need a 2-gallon (7.5-L) stockpot, a thermometer, a grain bag, a long spoon, a racking cane or siphon tube, a 2-gallon (7.5-L) brew bucket, a gallon (3.8-L) carboy and a bung and airlock.

2. Heat the water in the stockpot until it reaches 150 to 160°F (65 to 71°C). Pour the caramel and biscuit malt grains into the grain bag, tie a loose knot at the top and steep them in the pot for 20 minutes, while keeping the water temperature between 150 and 160°F (65 to 71°C). Remove the grain bag and let it drain back into the pot while you prepare for the next steps.

3. Bring your wort to a gentle, rolling boil. Add the dried malt extract and stir until the wort returns to a gentle boil. Add the Nugget hops and let those boil for 40 minutes. Add half of the Chinook hops and boil for 10 minutes. Add the remaining Chinook hops and boil another 10 minutes. Add the lemon zest and juice and black pepper. Fill a sink with ice water. Remove the pot from the heat and place it in the ice water in the sink. Let the wort cool until it is near 70°F (21°C).

4. Use the racking cane to siphon your wort into the bucket. Sprinkle the yeast into the wort and stir it. Put on the bucket lid, add the airlock, label your brew and store it in an area around 64 to 72°F (18 to 22°C) out of direct sunlight for 3 to 4 days.

5. Carefully transfer the beer into the jug, avoiding the lees at the bottom of the bucket. Return to the dark, warm place and wait for 2 weeks. Bottle (page 110) when ready.

RECIPE NOTE: Not happy with the lemon flavor at the time of bottling? Add lemon zest to your priming sugar while it simmers.

BASIL TRIPEL

A tripel is a strong pale ale. These Belgian beers tend to be golden, high in alcohol and on the sweet side of things, while remaining somehow light in body.

These complex beers undergo magic with aging in the bottle. While the basil notes are hardly detectable at the time of bottling, they rise and dance with the esters and floral notes of this heady herbal brew!

1½ gal (5.7 L) water

2 oz (55 g) Munich malt

20 oz (570 g) Pilsen light dried malt extract

8 g El Dorado hops pellets, divided

10 oz (280 g) Candi sugar

10 fresh basil leaves, sliced

1 tsp (2.5 g) Safale S-04 dry ale yeast

1. Gather your ingredients and sanitize your equipment. You'll need a 2-gallon (7.5-L) stockpot, a thermometer, a grain bag, a long spoon, a racking cane or siphon tube, a 2-gallon (7.5-L) brew bucket, a gallon (3.8-L) carboy and a bung and airlock.

2. Heat the water in the stockpot until it reaches 150 to 160°F (65 to 71°C). Pour the Munich malt grains into the grain bag, tie a loose knot at the top and steep them in the pot for 20 minutes, while keeping the temperature between 150 and 160°F (65 to 71°C). Remove the grain bag and let it drain back into the pot while you prepare for the next steps.

3. Bring your wort to a gentle, rolling boil. Add the dried malt extract and stir until the wort returns to a gentle boil. Add 5 grams of the El Dorado hops and let those boil for 30 minutes. Add the remaining 3 grams of hops and boil for another 15 minutes. Add the Candi sugar and simmer for a final 10 minutes. Add the sliced basil and stir, then cover the pot. Fill a sink with ice water. Remove the pot from the heat and place it in the ice water in the sink. Let the wort cool until it is near 70°F (21°C).

4. Use the racking cane to siphon your wort into the bucket. Sprinkle the yeast into the wort and stir it. Put on the bucket lid, add the airlock, label your brew and store it in an area around 64 to 72°F (18 to 22°C) out of direct sunlight for 3 to 4 days.

5. Carefully transfer the beer into the jug, avoiding the lees at the bottom of the bucket. Return to the dark, warm place and wait for 2 weeks. Bottle (page 110) when ready.

APRICOT AMERICAN WHEAT BEER

It is often encouraged to add fruit to beer during secondary fermentation: Primary fermentation will sometimes kill off the delicate aroma and flavors of fruit. You also run the risk of creating a pectin haze by adding the fruit during the boiling process.

The apricots used in this recipe are dried. Be sure that the apricots you buy are sulfite-free. They will be brown instead of the orange color that you might expect. Dried apricots that keep their color are processed with preservatives that will kill off your yeasts!

FOR THE BEER

1½ gal (5.7 L) water

4 oz (115 g) caramel 10L malt

1 lb (455 g) wheat dried malt extract

6 g El Dorado hops pellets, divided

1 tsp (2.5 g) Safale S-04 dry ale yeast

FOR RACKING

3½ oz (100 g) dried apricots, chopped

1. Gather your ingredients and sanitize your equipment. You'll need a 2-gallon (7.5-L) stockpot, a thermometer, a grain bag, a long spoon, a racking cane or siphon tube, a 2-gallon (7.5-L) brew bucket, a gallon (3.8-L) carboy and a bung and airlock.

2. For the beer, heat the water in the stockpot until it reaches 150 to 160°F (65 to 71°C). Pour the caramel malt grains into the grain bag, tie a loose knot at the top and steep them in the pot for 20 minutes, while keeping the temperature between 150 and 160°F (65 to 71°C). Remove the grain bag and let it drain back into the pot while you prepare for the next steps.

3. Bring your wort to a gentle, rolling boil. Add the dried malt extract and stir the wort until it returns to a gentle boil. Add half of the El Dorado hops and let those boil for 40 minutes. Add the remaining hops and boil another 20 minutes. Near the end of the boiling time, fill a sink with ice water. Remove the pot from the heat and place it in the ice water in the sink. Let the wort cool until it is near 70°F (21°C).

4. Use the racking cane to siphon your wort into the bucket. Sprinkle the yeast into the wort and stir it. Put on the bucket lid, add the airlock, label your brew and store it in an area around 64 to 72°F (18 to 22°C) out of direct sunlight for 3 to 4 days.

5. For racking, put the apricots in a blender with 1 to 2 cups (240 to 480 ml) of your beer. Blend into a frothy puree. Pour the puree into the gallon (3.8-L) jug. Carefully transfer the remaining beer onto the puree, avoiding the lees at the bottom of the bucket. Return to the dark, warm place and wait for 2 weeks. Bottle (page 110) when ready.

BLUEBERRY PORTER

Porter was my gateway beer back when I thought that I didn't care for hops. The rich, malty, smooth flavor of a chocolate porter quickly changed my mind!

While some people turn their nose up at fruity beers, the combination of dark porter and sweet blueberries is truly a match made in heaven. The blueberries are still present in the final palate, even though they are added during primary fermentation.

1½ gal (5.7 L) water

3 oz (85 g) Carapils malt

2 oz (55 g) chocolate malt

20 oz (570 g) amber dried malt extract

½ oz (14 g) Chinook hops pellets, divided

1 lb (455 g) frozen blueberries

1 tsp (2.5 g) Safale S-04 dry ale yeast

1. Gather your ingredients and sanitize your equipment. You'll need a 2-gallon (7.5-L) stockpot, a thermometer, a grain bag, a long spoon, a straining bag, a racking cane or siphon tube, a 2-gallon (7.5-L) brew bucket, a gallon (3.8-L) carboy and a bung and airlock.

2. Heat the water in the stockpot until it reaches 150 to 160°F (65 to 71°C). Pour the Carapils and chocolate malt grains into the grain bag, tie a loose knot at the top and steep them in the pot for 20 minutes, while keeping the temperature between 150 and 160°F (65 to 71°C). Remove the grain bag and let it drain back into the pot while you prepare for the next steps.

3. Bring your wort to a gentle, rolling boil. Add the dried malt extract and stir until the wort returns to a gentle boil. Add half of the hops and let those boil for 50 minutes. Add the remaining hops and boil for 10 minutes. Near the end of the boiling time, fill a sink with ice water. Remove the pot from the heat and place it in the ice water in the sink. Let the wort cool until it is near 70°F (21°C).

4. Put the blueberries in the straining bag and tie it shut. Place it in the bottom of the brew bucket and mash it gently with the spoon to release the juices.

5. Use the racking cane to siphon your wort into the bucket. Sprinkle the yeast into the wort and stir it. Put on the bucket lid, add the airlock, label your brew and store it in an area around 64 to 72°F (18 to 22°C) out of direct sunlight for 3 days. Make sure to pick up the bucket and give your beer a gentle swish every day to help inhibit mold growth on the surface of the brew.

6. Carefully transfer the beer into the jug, avoiding the lees at the bottom of the bucket. Let it work for another 2 weeks. Bottle (page 110) when ready.

ELDERFLOWER PALE ALE

Pale ale, the ubiquitous American style ale! This light beer has a nice balance of hops and malt, and while it is tasty, it is not what I would call remarkable.

Enter the elderflower. Prized for their delicate aroma and subtle floral notes, these lovely white flowers are the star of cordials, liqueurs and baked goods, and they make an excellent addition to a light beer, too!

1½ gal (5.7 L) water

4 oz (115 g) caramel 20L malt

20 oz (570 g) light dried malt extract

3 g El Dorado hops pellets

3 g Nugget hops pellets

3 g Lemondrop hops pellets

2 tbsp (5 g) dried elderflower

1 tsp (2.5 g) Safale S-04 dry ale yeast

1. Gather your ingredients and sanitize your equipment. You'll need a 2-gallon (7.5-L) stockpot, a thermometer, a grain bag, a long spoon, a racking cane or siphon tube, a 2-gallon (7.5-L) brew bucket, a gallon (3.8-L) carboy and a bung and airlock.

2. Heat the water in the stockpot until it reaches 150 to 160°F (65 to 71°C). Pour the caramel malt grains into the grain bag, tie a loose knot at the top and steep them in the pot for 30 minutes, while keeping the temperature between 150 and 160°F (65 to 71°C). Remove the grain bag and let it drain back into the pot while you prepare for the next steps.

3. Bring your wort to a gentle, rolling boil. Add the dried malt extract and stir the wort until it returns to a gentle boil. Add the El Dorado hops and boil for 40 minutes. Add the Nugget hops and boil another 10 minutes. Finally, add the Lemondrop hops and the elderflower and simmer for 5 more minutes. During the last 5 minutes of simmering, fill a sink with ice water. Remove the pot from the heat and place it in the ice water in the sink. Let the wort cool until it is near 70°F (21°C).

4. Use the racking cane to siphon your wort into the bucket, avoiding both the trub on the bottom and the dried elderflower floating on top. Sprinkle the yeast into the wort and stir it. Put on the bucket lid, add the airlock, label your brew and store it in an area around 64 to 72°F (18 to 22°C) out of direct sunlight for 3 to 4 days.

5. Carefully transfer the beer into the carboy, avoiding the lees at the bottom of the bucket. Return to the dark, warm place and wait for 2 weeks. Bottle (page 110) when ready.

DEEP ROOTS CHOCOLATE STOUT

As in the Root Beer Brown Ale (page 118), this recipe calls for some deep root tonic energies. In southern Appalachia, root tonics are traditionally taken early in the year, when fresh greens start to appear and young, tender roots can be dug for the table. These tonics are meant to stir the system, stimulate the body and help to flush out the stress and lethargy of winter.

This sturdy brew drinks like a meal! The earthy notes of the dandelion and burdock root are lifted from under the intense chocolate flavors by the aromatic licorice root. This combination makes for a balanced stout with some residual sweetness and a robust earthiness, ideal for the cold, wet nights of early spring.

1½ gal (5.7 L) water

4 oz (115 g) caramel 60L malt

2 oz (55 g) roasted barley malt

2 oz (55 g) Carapils malt

20 oz (570 g) amber dried malt extract

10 g El Dorado hops pellets, divided

1 tbsp (5 g) dried burdock root

1 tbsp (5 g) dried dandelion root

1 tsp (1 g) dried licorice root

1 oz (30 g) cacao nibs

2.5 g Safale S-04 dry ale yeast

1. Gather your ingredients and sanitize your equipment. You'll need a 2-gallon (7.5-L) stockpot, a thermometer, a grain bag, a long spoon, a racking cane or siphon tube, a 2-gallon (7.5-L) brew bucket, a gallon (3.8-L) carboy and a bung and airlock.

2. Heat the water in the stockpot until it reaches 150 to 160°F (65 to 71°C). Pour the caramel, roasted barley and Carapils malt grains into the grain bag, tie a loose knot at the top and steep them in the pot for 30 minutes, while keeping the temperature between 150 and 160°F (65 to 71°C). Remove the grain bag and let it drain back into the pot while you prepare for the next steps.

3. Bring your wort to a gentle, rolling boil. Add the dried malt extract and stir the wort until it returns to a gentle boil. Add 5 grams of the El Dorado hops and all of the burdock, dandelion and licorice roots, and let those boil for 40 minutes. Add the remaining 5 grams of the hops and boil another 10 minutes. Finally, add the cacao nibs and simmer for 10 more minutes. Near the end of the last 10 minutes of simmering, fill a sink with ice water. Remove the pot from the heat and place it in the ice water in the sink until it is near 70°F (21°C).

4. Use the racking cane to siphon your wort into the bucket, avoiding both the trub on the bottom and the roots floating on top. Sprinkle the yeast into the wort and stir it. Put on the bucket lid, add the airlock, label your brew and store it in an area around 64 to 72°F (18 to 22°C) out of direct sunlight for 3 to 4 days.

5. Carefully transfer the beer into the carboy, avoiding the lees at the bottom of the bucket. Return to the dark, warm place and wait for 2 weeks. Bottle (page 110) when ready.

MUGWORT BEER

This recipe is for another un-hopped beer done in an old-fashioned style. Mugwort has found its way into brews for centuries, and that is how it earned its name!

Mugwort is a potent herb. It has been taken internally and worn as a charm to increase instances of lucid dreaming and to help with divination. It has a mild psychoactive effect, as do many of the herbs commonly used in gruit. The bitters in mugwort help to stimulate the digestive system, encourage sweating and urination and, interestingly, acts both as a mild stimulant and as a nervine to calm jangled nerves.

1½ gal (5.7 L) water

20 oz (570 g) Pilsen light dried malt extract

2 lemons, chopped

1 oz (30 g) dried mugwort

5 oz (141 g) molasses

2 tbsp (40 g) honey

1 tsp (2.5 g) pale ale yeast

1.　Gather your ingredients and sanitize your equipment. You'll need a 2-gallon (7.5-L) stockpot, a long spoon, a thermometer, a racking cane or siphon tube, a 2-gallon (7.5-L) brew bucket, a gallon (3.8-L) carboy and a bung and airlock.

2.　Bring the water to a boil and stir in the dried malt extract. Let the water return to a boil and add the lemons, the mugwort and the molasses. Let the wort simmer at a gentle boil for 30 minutes. Near the end of the 30 minutes, fill a sink with ice water. Stir in the honey. Remove the pot from the heat, and place it in the ice water in the sink. Let the wort cool until it is near 70°F (21°C).

3.　Use the racking cane to siphon the wort into the bucket, avoiding transferring the herbal sludge from the brew pot. Sprinkle the yeast into the wort and stir it. Put on the bucket lid, add the airlock, label your brew and store it in an area around 64 to 72°F (18 to 22°C) out of direct sunlight for 4 to 6 days.

4.　Carefully transfer the beer into the carboy, again avoiding the lees at the bottom of the bucket. Return the jug to the dark, warm place and wait for 2 weeks. Bottle (page 110) when ready.

RECIPE NOTE: Like the gruit ale, this is not traditionally carbonated, although you can add priming sugar (page 110) during bottling if you wish. I prefer the still, heady mugwort brew without all of the bubbles!

BRAGGOT

A cross between mead and beer, a braggot has honey and malt as the main fermentable sugars. This is another one of those brews that defy exact understanding of where it comes from, nor is there a steadfast recipe by which it is made! This recipe is heavy on the honey, but with enough malt that the end result should be a well-balanced brew with a rich sweetness and a light, malty finish.

1 gal (3.8 L) water, divided

1 lb (455 g) golden light dried malt extract

3 lb (1.4 kg) honey

1 tsp (2.5 g) Safale S-04 dry ale yeast

1. Gather your ingredients and sanitize your supplies. You'll need a 1- or 2-gallon (3.8- or 7.6-L) stockpot, a thermometer, a long spoon, a funnel and strainer, a gallon (3.8-L) carboy and a bung and airlock.

2. Heat ⅔ gallon (2.5 L) of the water to just about boiling. Pour in the dried malt extract and stir until it is completely dissolved. Remove the pot from the heat and add the honey. Once the mixture is well blended, let it sit for another 10 minutes or so to cool.

3. Use the funnel and strainer to pour the warm brew into the gallon (3.8-L) carboy. Top off the carboy with as much of the remaining ⅓ gallon (1.3 L) of water needed for the must to reach the neck of the jug. Seal the jug with the bung and airlock to keep everything clean.

4. Allow the must to cool until it reaches 90°F (32°C); this can take a few hours. Once the glass is cool enough that you can touch the jug on the bottom and not feel the heat, you can pitch the yeast. Reseal the jug. Pick it up and give the jug a good shake for a few minutes to mix in the yeast and oxygen, and then recap the carboy with the bung and airlock.

5. Label the jug with the brew name and date and set it aside somewhere out of direct sunlight and let it do its fermenting magic!

6. You can bottle this still or carbonate it using priming sugar (page 110).

Beyond the Brews

Once you have become a homebrewer and built a well-stocked larder of brews that would do any hobbit proud, you are faced with the task of using up the brews! Tasting parties are fun, but there is something especially lovely when you pair the beer you are tasting with crackers made from its spent grain. There's nothing more pleasant than a glass of stout and a slice of stout ginger bread on a winter's night.

Cocktails

It's a delight to be able to create a brew from scratch, but you can take it a bit further by turning your wine, beer, mead and cider into a cocktail! Try using an alcoholic ginger brew in place of ginger soda to make a dark and stormy with an extra kick, or use cider and beer with complementary flavors to pour a Snakebite.

Your creativity and tastes are the limits of what you can do to mix a new drink from one of your homebrews! Here are a few simple recipes to get you started.

MEAD SPRITZER

YIELD VARIES

Sometimes a batch of mead, wine or cider will turn out a bit too sweet or too dry for your liking. Don't worry; all is not lost! You can use mixers to make your brew more palatable and transform them into bubbling cocktails.

IF YOUR BREW IS TOO SWEET

2 parts sweet brew

1 part soda water, mineral water or fruit-flavored, unsweetened soda

IF YOUR BREW IS TOO DRY

2 parts dry brew

1 part ginger ale or sweetened citrus soda

1. For brew that is too sweet, mix the correct ratio of sweet brew to soda water. Make it fancy by serving it on the rocks with a sprig of fresh herbs or edible flowers from the garden.

2. For brew that is too dry, a spoonful of sugar makes the medicine go down, right? Mix the correct ratio of dry brew to ginger ale to give your brew new life!

MULLED MEAD, WINE AND CIDER

SERVES 1

There's nothing quite like enjoying the first few crisp nights of autumn with a cup of warm, spiced cheer to keep you company! It is so easy to mull mead, wine or cider that you'll wonder why you never tried it before.

Here are a few examples to get you started. Each recipe is for a single cup of mulled brew.

MULLED RED WINE OR CIDER

1 cup (240 ml) red wine or cider

1 stick cinnamon

2 cardamom seeds

3 crushed grains of paradise

Brown sugar or honey, to taste

MULLED MEAD OR WHITE WINE

1 cup (240 ml) mead or white wine

1 tsp crushed dried rose hips

0.04 oz (2 g) fresh ginger, thinly sliced

1 dried or fresh orange slice

Honey, to taste

1. Mix your mead, wine or cider with a few simple ingredients on a pot on the stove. These recipe suggestions are for one serving, but you can scale it up as much as needed to serve a crowd. Warm the brew and the spices at a low temperature. Don't let it boil! It just needs to be warm enough to let the spices infuse, but not so hot that the alcohol is burned away. The longer you wait, the better the result. You can enjoy a cup of mulled wine after 30 minutes or so, but give it a few hours to really let the flavors blend.

TIPS: You can make a batch of mulled mead or wine in advance of fall—return the mulled beverage to a swing-top bottle and store the spiced, sweetened brew until you need it. If you feel yourself coming down with a cold, warm a cup of mulled spice wine and you'll be all set to bundle up for bedtime.

Consider other spices, such as chamomile, licorice root, black pepper, nutmeg, garam masala or cayenne. The sky is the limit!

Simple Syrups

There is another way to brighten up a dry wine, mead or cider. Imagine that a sweet wine has turned to a bubbling, dry brew when you open a bottle later on. The floral flavors that it once had seem to be lost—but don't despair! A touch of simple syrup added to a glass of your dry brew can revive those delicate touches.

If this simple syrup is too simple for you, try the following variations and then experiment with your own ideas!

BASIC SIMPLE SYRUP

YIELD VARIES

You can scale this recipe to create as much simple syrup as you need. One cup of each ingredient (240 ml water, and 200 g sugar or 340 g honey) is usually more than enough to "fix" a bottle of dry wine.

1 part sugar or honey

1 part water

1. Sanitize a bottle. Mix the sugar and water in a saucepan and cook over medium heat, stirring to ensure that the sugar is completely dissolved. Bring the mixture to a boil for 1 minute. Remove the pan from the heat and allow the syrup to cool before pouring it into the bottle. Label the syrup and refrigerate it for up to 6 months.

GINGER-HONEY SYRUP

MAKES 2½ CUPS (600 ML)

Stir a spoonful of this syrup into any hot drink to kick it up a notch—tea, spiced chai or a mulled cider.

1 cup (240 ml) water

½ cup (50 g) grated fresh ginger

1 cup (340 g) honey

1.   Sanitize a bottle. In a small saucepan, bring the water and ginger to boil over medium heat. Reduce the heat to low and allow the mixture to simmer for 5 minutes, and then stir in the honey.

2.   Allow the syrup to boil for 1 minute, then remove it from the heat and let it cool. Strain the ginger out, pour the syrup into the bottle and label. Store the syrup in the refrigerator for up to 6 months.

CINNAMON-BROWN SUGAR SYRUP

MAKES 2 CUPS (480 ML)

This is not only wonderful drizzled over cake or into a banana smoothie, it is also a rock star when paired with Maple Syrup Cider (page 92).

1 cup (240 ml) water

1–2 sticks cinnamon (to your taste)

1 cup (200 g) packed brown sugar

1. Sanitize a bottle. In a small saucepan, bring the water and cinnamon sticks to a boil over medium heat. Gently stir in the brown sugar until it has completely dissolved.

2. Allow the mixture to return to a boil for 1 minute and then remove it from the heat. Once it has cooled off, pour the syrup and cinnamon sticks into the bottle. Don't forget to label and date the bottle! Store the syrup in the refrigerator for up to 6 months.

Cooking with Homebrews

Your best beers get consumed with great gusto, but then there's the matter of brews that you don't quite like. Baking and cooking with those lackluster ciders, bitter beers or overly sweet meads gives us a way to use them up without wasting them. One perk to brewing all-grain beer is that you get to use the spent grains left after brew day! The humble little bag of wet grains can be used in many ways. Try making breads, flours, dog treats, granola or muffins with this high-fiber grain. Don't feel like baking? If you are on a homestead, use spent grains as a favorite snack for chickens and livestock, or use them to enrich your compost pile.

SPENT-GRAIN FLOUR

YIELD VARIES

Spent grains can be dried and milled into flour. Not unlike a rye flour, this has a dark and nutty flavor with a slight residual sweetness. It's a healthy addition to baking, as it is high in fiber, protein and amino acids. Spent-grain flour can be used in recipes along with all-purpose flour. For example, substitute 1 cup (140 g) of whole wheat flour with ½ cup (70 g) of spent-grain flour and ½ cup (70 g) of all-purpose flour.

Spent grains as available

1. After making the wort on brew day, take a few minutes to pour your wet grains into a strainer in the sink. Let them drip dry while you finish brewing.

2. Arrange the wet grains in a shallow layer on a dehydrator tray or a shallow rimmed baking sheet and put them in the dehydrator or the oven, ideally at a temperature of around 150°F (65°C). Check on them every hour and stir, so that they dry evenly without burning. It should take 2 to 4 hours for the grain to be totally dried. You can tell your grains are done because they will be crisp and warm with no trace of moisture remaining.

3. Remove the grains from the heat source and let them cool. Pulse the dried grains in a food processor or spice grinder. It will take about 30 seconds worth of grinding to get the grains fine enough to store.

4. Store your flour in an airtight container in a dark cabinet. If you don't bake often, store the flour in the freezer to extend its shelf life.

HERBED SPENT-GRAIN CRACKERS

MAKES ABOUT 3 DOZEN 2-INCH (5-CM) CRACKERS

What better way to use an abundance of spent grain than to make a snack to pair with your beer? These crackers are strong, crispy and full of flavor. They make an ideal companion for a cheese tray when paired with a sharp, crumbly cheddar.

What herbs do you have in abundance? This recipe is very flexible, so instead of the thyme and oregano, try with rosemary, tarragon, parsley or cilantro—any culinary herb will do!

1¼ cups (175 g) all-purpose flour

¾ cup (105 g) spent-grain flour (page 148)

2 tsp (9 g) baking powder

1 tsp sea salt, plus more to taste

½ tsp black pepper

2 tsp (2 g) chopped fresh thyme

2 tsp (2 g) chopped fresh oregano

2 tsp (6 g) garlic powder

3 tbsp (45 ml) olive oil

¼ cup (60 ml) water

Freshly ground back pepper

1. Preheat the oven to 375°F (190°C).

2. Mix the all-purpose and spent-grain flour, baking powder, salt, pepper, thyme, oregano and garlic powder. Drizzle in the olive oil and slowly add the water. Stir until it forms a soft, sticky dough, adding more water a bit at a time, if needed.

3. Lightly flour a sheet of parchment paper or a silicone baking sheet. With a rolling pin, roll the dough to a thickness of ⅛ inch (3 mm). Use a knife or cookie cutter to cut the dough into shapes. I rough-cut my crackers in some round and some square shapes to make them rustic.

4. Use a fork to poke holes in the crackers. This will make sure that they crisp up rather than rise and become chewy. Sprinkle the tops of the crackers with salt and a bit of pepper.

5. Bake the crackers for 13 to 15 minutes, or until they are golden brown. Let them cool on the pan, as that will help them crisp up. Store the crackers in an airtight container for up to 2 weeks.

VARIATIONS ON A THEME: Why stop at sea salt? Top your crackers with sesame seeds, flaxseeds, Parmesan cheese, cracked wheat berries or whatever strikes your fancy!

SPENT-GRAIN GRANOLA

MAKES 5 CUPS (1 KG)

If you like granola, but you have never tried making your own, wait until you taste this!
It is so delicious right out of the oven that we don't always have any left to store. Try this granola
served over skyr or another thick yogurt with fresh fruit for a hearty, healthy snack.

1½ cups (180 g) dried spent grain

1½ cups (140 g) rolled oats

1 cup (120 g) raw pecans, chopped into large pieces

½ cup (60 g) slivered almonds

½ cup (30 g) unsweetened flaked coconut

1 tbsp (10 g) flaxseeds

1 tbsp (10 g) hemp seeds

½ cup (120 ml) coconut oil, melted

⅓ cup (80 ml) maple syrup

⅓ cup (115 g) honey

¼ tsp ground cinnamon

⅛ tsp ground ginger

¼ tsp sea salt, divided

¼ cup (35 g) chopped dried fruit or (45 g) chocolate or yogurt chips, optional

1. Preheat the oven to 300°F (150°C). Line a baking pan with parchment paper or a silicone mat.

2. In a large bowl, mix the dried spent grain, rolled oats, pecans, almonds, coconut, flaxseeds and hemp seeds. Drizzle the coconut oil, maple syrup and honey over the dry ingredients and stir to blend. Sprinkle in the cinnamon, ginger and half of the salt. Stir to mix; add as much of the remaining salt as you desire.

3. Spread the granola in a thin layer on the baking pan. Bake for 30 to 40 minutes, turning the granola every 10 minutes to prevent burning. When the granola is golden brown, transfer the pan from the oven to a wire rack.

4. Cool completely. If using dried fruit, transfer the granola to a large bowl and stir it in.

5. Store the granola in an airtight container and use within a week or so—but I've never had it stay around that long!

SPENT-GRAIN BEER BREAD

This recipe is for a quick bread, or a bread that doesn't require yeast and a long wait for it to rise. Quick breads are denser and moister than their yeasted counterparts. The baking powder and beer are the rising agents in this tasty, versatile recipe.

3 tbsp (45 g) sugar, plus more to dust the pan

1½ cups (180 g) spent-grain flour (page 148)

1½ cups (180 g) all-purpose flour

1½ tsp (9 g) sea salt

1 tbsp (11 g) baking powder

1½ cups (360 ml) beer

1. Preheat the oven to 375°F (190°C) and grease a loaf pan. If desired, sprinkle a little sugar into the greased pan to give your bread a crisp, sugary crust.

2. In a large bowl, mix the spent-grain flour, all-purpose flour, salt, sugar and baking powder. Make a well in the center of the dry ingredients and slowly pour in the beer. Stir well until all of the elements are moist and well distributed.

3. Pour the batter into the pan and bake for 45 to 60 minutes, or until a toothpick inserted into the center comes out clean.

4. Remove the bread from the oven and transfer it to a wire rack when the pan is cool enough to handle. Cool the bread completely before slicing.

VARIATIONS ON A THEME: This recipe is malleable! Add spices and seasonings to accentuate the flavor of the beer that you are using in the recipe. For example, try black pepper, oregano or thyme, or grate a hard cheese into the dough for a bread made with an IPA or pale ale. If you are using a stout or porter, consider adding a spoonful of sugar, molasses and ginger or some dried fruit. The possibilities are endless!

MARINADES AND SAUCES

Now that you have a cabinet full of homebrewed goodies, you can get creative in the kitchen! This easy-to-follow formula creates a delicious marinade for meats and veggies.

1 cup (240 ml) wine, mead, cider or beer

½ cup (120 ml) light oil, such as extra virgin olive oil or walnut oil, or melted butter

Fresh herbs and spices, mustard, citrus juice and other seasonings, to taste

1 tsp salt

1. Whisk together the wine, oil, herbs and spices and salt.

2. Arrange the meat or vegetables in a shallow baking pan and pour the marinade over it. Cover the dish and marinate the chicken, seafood or vegetables in the refrigerator for up to 3 hours. You can marinate beef in the refrigerator for up to 24 hours.

HERE ARE SOME EXAMPLES OF HOW YOU CAN APPLY THE MARINADE FORMULA:

- Spiced Pomegranate Wine (page 57) with extra virgin olive oil, thyme, oregano, black pepper, garlic and salt for spiced beef, mushrooms or eggplant.

- Maple Syrup Cider (page 92) with browned butter, nutmeg, cloves, brown sugar and salt for a pork shoulder.

- Lemon-Pepper IPA (page 121) with extra virgin olive oil, fresh lemon juice, rosemary and salt for grilled chicken or fish.

TURN YOUR MARINADE INTO A SAUCE: After draining the meat or vegetables, bring the used marinade to a boil for 1 minute, and then simmer it for 3 minutes to reduce it into a sauce that you can serve with the meal.

VINAIGRETTES

Put your brews to use in another versatile style of condiment: salad vinaigrette! Your ciders, meads and wines can make your dinner shine if you follow the formula. Don't be afraid to get creative! "Other seasonings to taste" is a broad direction, and I mean it. You can use mustard, Worcestershire sauce, honey, tahini, tamari, miso, wasabi, sriracha, jelly, sugar or molasses. Make this recipe your own!

¾ cup (180 ml) light oil, such as extra virgin olive oil or walnut oil

¼ cup (60 ml) wine, mead, cider or vinegar

Spices, citrus juice or other seasonings to taste

1.   In a blender, mix the oil, wine and seasonings until well combined.

HERE ARE SOME EXAMPLES OF HOW YOU CAN APPLY THE MARINADE FORMULA:

*   Lemon and Ginger Mead (page 40) with sesame oil, freshly squeezed lemon, salt and pepper.

*   Raspberry-Pear Wine (page 77) with walnut oil, mustard and salt.

*   Summer Berry Cider (page 96) with extra virgin olive oil, garam masala and salt.

BOOZY JELLIES

This small-batch recipe will guide you through making a lovely jelly from your homebrew.
It will work with cider, mead or wine—consider the possibilities! You can store these jellies in the freezer
or process them in a boiling water bath to make them shelf stable for up to a year.

2 cups (480 ml) mead, wine or cider
1½ lb (680 g) sugar
1 (3-oz [90-ml]) packet liquid pectin

1. Sanitize four 8-ounce (250-ml) jelly jars and their lids. If you are going to be canning the jelly, use brand new lids and bands.

2. Pour the mead into a saucepan. Add the sugar, stirring until it is completely dissolved. Let the mixture come to a rolling boil and add the liquid pectin. Keep stirring until the liquid returns to a boil for a full minute. Remove from the heat immediately.

3. Ladle the jelly into the jars, leaving ½ inch (1.3 cm) of headspace. Cap the jars with the lids. To keep them shelf-stable, process them in a water bath according to the directions on your package of pectin. Otherwise, label them with the date after they cool and store them in the freezer. Whatever method you use, it is best to let the jars cool before you move them, as this helps the jelly to set.

CIDER-POACHED PEARS

SERVES 4

Poached pears make a beautiful dessert as is, but they also make a fantastic topping for waffles, ice cream or a bowl of creamy yogurt with Spent-Grain Granola (page 152).

1 cup (240 ml) apple cider

½ tsp garam masala

¼ tsp ground ginger

2 ripe, firm pears, peeled, cored and halved lengthwise

¼ cup (50 g) packed brown sugar

1. In a large skillet, bring the apple cider, garam masala and ginger to a boil over high heat. Gently place the pears into the simmering syrup.

2. Reduce the heat to low and continue to simmer the pears for about 20 minutes, or until they are tender. With a slotted spoon, carefully remove the pears from the pan to a bowl. Cover the bowl with aluminum foil to keep the pears warm.

3. Turn up the heat on the skillet, add the brown sugar and boil, stirring constantly for about 2 minutes, or until the cider has reduced to a syrup.

4. Serve the pears warm with cider syrup spooned over them!

TIP: A melon baller makes it easy to core fruit.

FRUIT-SCRAP VINEGAR

YIELD VARIES

When you are processing fresh apples or pears to make cider, you'll end up with fruit that didn't make the cut. Bruised or damaged fruit can make a cider taste bad, but don't worry—that culled fruit is perfect for creating a batch of your own vinegar!

Vinegar-making is surprisingly easy. All you need is a liquid that is fermented and a "mother of vinegar." You can purchase a packet or tube of vinegar mother from a homesteading shop, but you can also use Bragg or a similar live apple cider vinegar to use as a starter.

Chopped apple or pear scraps (peels, cores and bruised bits)

Sufficient jars or crocks to contain the fruit

Sugar, optional

Mother of vinegar

1. Roughly chop the fruit and peels and place them in the jars or crocks—skin, core, peel and all. A gallon (3.8-L) pickle jar works well, but any jar or pot that will fit the amount of fruit you have should do just fine! If you wish, you can layer your fruit with a bit of sugar to help release the juices, but it is not necessary for the flavor or a successful fermentation.

2. Pour water over the fruit until it is just covered. Cap your fermenting jar with a piece of cloth, secured with a tie or rubber band. The cloth will allow the brew to breathe as it begins to ferment and keep out dust and bugs.

3. Set the jar aside on your counter or in a cabinet. You want to keep it in a spot out of direct sunlight, but don't forget about it! After a day or 2, little bubbles will appear as the fruit and water begin fermenting. Give it one more day after you notice the bubbles and then strain the solids out, returning the bubbly liquid to a clean, wide-mouthed jar or crock.

4. Add the mother of vinegar. If you are using a live vinegar that you already have, shake up the bottle to mix it well and pour about 1 tablespoon (15 ml) of the vinegar into the fermenting jar. If you purchased a mother of vinegar culture, follow the suggestions on the package for adding it in.

5. Cover the jar or crock with a new, clean cloth and rubber band because fruit flies are going to be very excited about your new project. Keep an eye on the jar to make sure they can't get in!

(continued)

6. After a day or so, you'll see white, ghostly oil slicks appear on the surface of the liquid. They will continue to grow until you have a healthy mother of vinegar. The vinegar mother looks like a white, translucent, rubbery plug on the top of the ferment. Once the mother is solidly established and protecting the vinegar, move the jug to a cool, dark area and let it sit for at least a month.

7. When you are ready to bottle the vinegar, gently pour off the liquid through a strainer and into a large bowl with a spout, and from there into sanitized bottles. Label and store those bottles in a dark spot for later use. A little skin of mother might grow in the neck of the bottle, which is fine. Just shake it up before use!

8. Meanwhile, you can leave the mother and enough liquid to cover her in the jar if you think you'll be making another batch soon. A cloth-covered vinegar mother can live on your counter like a sourdough starter. Whenever you have a bit of homebrewed wine, mead or other live-fermented liquid, give her a splash of it to keep her fed until you use her again. You can also cut her into pieces and share her with friends!

9. You can safely consume the vinegar as soon as it is bottled, but you should stash a few bottles away for at least 2 years to allow the mellow, fruity flavors time to develop. It's worth the wait!

ACKNOWLEDGMENTS

To the loves of my life: Eric and our baby Alia, who was born three months before the manuscript was due! Thank you for your patience, support and hard work to help me finish this book.

To my teachers: Kevin Kelley, master meadmaker; Jeff Spurlin, beer brewer and punster extraordinaire; and Margo "Owl" Crim, and her rich, sweet wines.

To Colleen Codekas, for helping to connect me to Page Street Publishing, and for being a wonderful creative ally in the herbal community.

To Jen CK Jacobs, for her amazing photography and food styling skills, and for being a breeze to work with. A dream come true!

To Page Street Publishing, for having a vision for what we could create together and offering me this amazing opportunity. Sarah (congratulations!), Karen, Meg and everyone involved has been a delight.

ABOUT THE AUTHOR

AMBER SHEHAN is an herbalist and the creator of Pixie's Pocket. She lives in the glorious Appalachian Mountains near Asheville, North Carolina, with her own true love Eric and wee baby Alia, a dog, a cat and a few chickens. Their yard full of herbs, weeds and wildflowers gets turned into medicines, meads and other wonderfully weird brews.

INDEX

airlock, 14

ale
  Basil Tripel, 122
  cherry red, 114
  elderflower pale, 129
  gruit, 113
  root beer brown, 118

American Pilsner, 109–110

apples, 81
  See also cider
  apple mead, 47
  Fruit-Scrap Vinegar, 164–166

apricots
  Apricot American Wheat Beer, 125
  Fruitcake Wine, 74

backsweetening, 19

Basic Simple Syrup, 143

Basil Tripel, 122

batch size, 12

Bavarian Purity Laws, 107

beer, 106–135
  Apricot American Wheat Beer, 125
  Basil Tripel, 122

Blueberry Porter, 126

Braggot, 134

brewing, 106–107

Cherry Red Ale, 114

Deep Roots Chocolate Stout, 130

Elderflower Pale Ale, 129

Gruit Ale, 113

ingredients, 107

Lemon-Pepper IPA, 121

Master Recipe: American Pilsner, 109–110

mugwort, 133

Root Beer Brown Ale, 118

Thyme and Honey Saison, 117

beer bottles, 15–16

Beer Bread, Spent-Grain, 155

bees, 21

berries
  Blueberry Muffin Mead, 31
  Blueberry Porter, 126
  Elderberry and Rose Hip Wine, 65
  Gruit Ale, 113
  raspberry honey, 21
  Raspberry-Pear Wine, 77
  Strawberry and Linden Flower Wine, 66
  Summer Berry Cider, 96

bilbemel mead, 31

bittering agents, 107, 113

Black Cherry Mead, 43

black tea, 18

bleach, 14

blueberries

    Blueberry Muffin Mead, 31

    Blueberry Porter, 126

Boozy Jellies, 160

bottles, 15–16

bottling, 19

Braggot, 134

Bread, Spent-Grain Beer, 155

brewing

    basics, 11

    equipment, 12–16

    ingredients, 16–18

    process, 18–19

    small batches, 12

brewing community, 11

brewing pot, 13

bung, 14

burdock root, 130

calendula flowers, Flower Garden Cider, 100

caps, 15–16

Chai-Spiced Cider, 95

chamomile

    Flower Garden Cider, 100

    Vanilla Bean and Chamomile Mead, 39

cheesecloth, 16

cherries

    Black Cherry Mead, 43

    Cherry Red Ale, 114

    Chocolate-Cherry Wine, 78

    Fruitcake Wine, 74

chlorine, 16

chocolate

    Chocolate-Cherry Wine, 78

    Deep Roots Chocolate Stout, 130

cider, 80–105

    chai-spiced, 95

    Cider-Poached Pears, 163

    dark ginger, 91

    dry-hopped, 99

    flower garden, 100

    malted, 104

    maple syrup, 92

    master recipe, 83–84

    mulled, 140

    orange-hibiscus, 88

    perry (pear), 87

    rose, 103

    summer berry, 96

    yeast for, 81

Cinnamon-Brown Sugar Syrup, 147

citric acid, 81

Clementine Mead, Rosemary and, 32

clover honey, 21

Cocktails, 139–140

corked bottles, 19

corks, 15–16

country wines, 51

Crackers, Herbed Spent-Grain, 151

Cyser (Apple Mead), 47

damiana, Honeymoon Mead, 44

dandelion root, 130

Deep Roots Chocolate Stout, 130

digital scale, 13

dogs, 107

dried flowers/herbs, 17, 36

drinking, 19

Dry-Hopped Cider, 99

Earl Grey Tea Wine, 73

Elderberry and Rose Hip Wine, 65

Elderflower Pale Ale, 129

equipment, 12–16

fermenter, 14

Flour, Spent-Grain, 148

flowers, 17

    dried, 17, 36

    Elderberry and Rose Hip Wine, 65

    Elderflower Pale Ale, 129

    Flower Garden Cider, 100

    Rose Cider, 103

    Rose Petal and Hibiscus Mead, 36

    Strawberry and Linden Flower Wine, 66

    Vanilla Bean and Chamomile Mead, 39

    wildflower honey, 21

    Wildflower Mead, 28

foraging, 17

forums, 12

Fruitcake Wine, 74

Fruit-Scrap Vinegar, 164

fruit wine

    See also wine

    master recipe, 53–54

funnels, 16

Ginger

    Chai-Spiced Cider, 95

    Dark Ginger Cider, 91

    Ginger-Honey Syrup, 144

    Golden Mead, 35

    Lemon and Ginger Mead, 40

Golden Mead, 35

golden milk, 35

grain of paradise, 114

Granola, Spent-Grain, 152

grapefruit

    Wildflower Mead, 28

    wine, 69

grapes, 51

    Fruit Wine, Master Recipe, 53–54

    Grape Mead, 48

grolsch bottles, 15

Gruit Ale, 113

gruits, 107

hedgerow wines, 51

herbal wines, 51, 70

Herbed Spent-Grain Crackers, 151

herbs, 17, 36, 107

hibiscus

    Orange-Hibiscus Cider, 88

    Rose Petal and Hibiscus Mead, 36

honey, 21

    See also mead

    Ginger-Honey Syrup, 144

Honeymoon Mead, 44

Honeysuckle Wine, 61

hops, 107

    Dry-Hopped Cider, 99

ingredients, 16–18

IPA, Lemon-Pepper, 121

Jellies, Boozy, 160

juniper berries, Gruit Ale, 113

Lady Grey Tea Wine, 73

lemon

    Lemon and Ginger Mead, 40

    Lemon Balm Mead, 27

    Lemon-Pepper IPA, 121

licorice root, 130

Linden Flower Wine, Strawberry and, 66

Malted Cider, 104

Maple Syrup Cider, 92

Marinades, 156

master recipes

    American pilsner, 109–110

    cider, 83–84

    mead, 22–23

    wine, 53–54

mead, 20–49

    black cherry, 43

    blueberry muffin, 31

    cyser (apple), 47

    golden, 35

    honey for, 21

    honeymoon, 44

    lemon and ginger, 40

    lemon balm, 27

    master recipe, 22–23

    mead spritzer, 139

    mulled, 140

    pyment (grape), 48

    rosemary and clementine, 32

    rose petal and hibiscus, 36

    storage of, 19

    vanilla bean and chamomile, 39

    wildflower, 28

Mugwort Beer, 133

Mulled Mead, Wine and Cider, 140

oats, Spent-Grain Granola, 152
One Step, 14
orange blossom honey, 21
Orange-Hibiscus Cider, 88

Pear Cider, 87
pears, 81
    cider-poached, 163
    Fruit-Scrap Vinegar, 164–166
    Raspberry-Pear Wine, 77
Peppermint Wine, 62
Perry (Pear Cider), 87
Pilsner, American, 109–110
Pineapple Wine, 58
Pomegranate Wine, Spiced, 57
Porter, Blueberry, 126
potassium sorbate, 19, 54
Pyment (Grape Mead), 48

racking, 19
racking cane, 15
raisins
    Fruitcake Wine, 74
    as yeast nutrient, 17

raspberries
    raspberry honey, 21
    Raspberry-Pear Wine, 77
Root Beer Brown Ale, 118
Rose Hip Wine, Elderberry and, 65
rosemary
    Rosemary and Clementine Mead, 32
    Scarborough Fair Wine, 70
rose petals
    Flower Garden Cider, 100
    Rose Cider, 103
    Rose Petal and Hibiscus Mead, 36

Sage, Scarborough Fair Wine, 70
Saison, Thyme and Honey, 117
sanitized straw, 15
sanitizer, 14
sarsaparilla, 118
sassafras, 118
Sauces, 156
Scarborough Fair Wine, 70
Simple Syrups, 143–147
siphon tube, 15
sourwood honey, 21
spent grain
    Herbed Spent-Grain Crackers, 151
    Spent-Grain Beer Bread, 155
    Spent-Grain Flour, 148
    Spent-Grain Granola, 152
spoons, 14

storage, 19

strainer, 16

straining bags, 16

Strawberry and Linden Flower Wine, 66

sugars, 19, 51, 54

Summer Berry Cider, 96

swing-top bottles, 15

tannins, 18

tasting, 18

tea

    black, 18

    Earl Grey Tea Wine, 73

    Lady Grey Tea Wine, 73

thermometer, 13

thyme

    Scarborough Fair Wine, 70

    Thyme and Honey Saison, 117

time, for fermentation, 18

Tripel, Basil, 122

tubing, 15

turmeric, Golden Mead, 35

Vanilla Bean and Chamomile Mead, 39

Vinaigrettes, 159

Vinegar, Fruit-Scrap, 164–166

water, 16

Wheat Beer, Apricot American, 125

wildflower honey, 21

Wildflower Mead, 28

wine, 50–79

    about, 51

    chocolate-cherry, 78

    Earl Grey tea, 73

    elderberry and rose hip, 65

    fruitcake, 74

    grapefruit, 69

    hedgerow, 51

    herbal, 51, 70

    honeysuckle, 61

    Lady Grey tea, 73

    Master Recipe: Fruit Wine, 53–54

    mulled, 140

    peppermint, 62

    pineapple, 58

    raspberry-pear, 77

    Scarborough Fair, 70

    Spiced Pomegranate, 57

    storage of, 19

    Strawberry and Linden Flower, 66

wine bottles, 15

wine thief, 15

yarrow

    Flower Garden Cider, 100

    Gruit Ale, 113

yeast, 17, 81

yeast nutrient, 17, 19